2010 SUPPLEMENT

CASES AND MATERIALS

EMPLOYMENT LAW

SIXTH EDITION

by

MARK A. ROTHSTEIN
Herbert F. Boehl Chair of Law and Medicine
University of Louisville

LANCE LIEBMAN
William S. Beinecke Professor of Law
Columbia University

FOUNDATION PRESS
2010

THOMSON REUTERS

© 2008, 2009 THOMSON REUTERS/FOUNDATION PRESS

© 2010 By THOMSON REUTERS/FOUNDATION PRESS

     1 New York Plaza, 34th Floor

     New York, NY 10004

     Phone Toll Free 1–877–888–1330

     Fax (646) 424–5201

     foundation–press.com

Printed in the United States of America

ISBN 978–1–59941–819–3

Mat #40979837

TABLE OF CONTENTS

TABLE OF CASES

Principal cases are in bold type. Non-principal cases are in roman type. References are to Pages.

2010 SUPPLEMENT

CASES AND MATERIALS

EMPLOYMENT LAW

PART I

BACKGROUND

CHAPTER 1

WORK AND LAW

A.   WORK AND SOCIETY

Page 8.   Please delete the Terkel excerpt and replace it with the following.

Steven Greenhouse, The Big Squeeze: Tough Times for the American Worker

3–5 (2008).

In his job at Wal–Mart in Texas, Mike Mitchell was responsible for catching shoplifters, and he was good at it, too, catching 180 in one two-year period. But one afternoon things went wildly awry when he chased a thief—a woman using stolen checks—into the parking lot. She jumped into her car, and her accomplice gunned the accelerator, slamming the car into Mitchell and sending him to the hospital with a broken kneecap, badly torn shoulder, and two herniated disks. Mitchell was so devoted to Wal–Mart that he somehow returned to work the next day, but a few weeks later he told his boss that he needed surgery on his knee. He was fired soon

1

afterward, apparently as part of a strategy to dismiss workers whose injuries run up Wal–Mart's workers' comp bills.

* * *

Immediately after serving in the army, Dawn Eubanks took a seven-dollar-an-hour job at a call center in Florida. Some days she was told to clock in just two or three hours, and some days she was not allowed to clock in during her whole eight-hour shift. The call center's managers warned the workers that if they went home, even though they weren't allowed to clock in, they would be viewed as having quit.

* * *

Twenty-eight-year-old John Arnold works in the same Caterpillar factory in Illinois as his father, but under the plant's two-tier contract, the maximum he can ever earn is $14.90 an hour, far less than the $25 earned by his father. Caterpillar, long a symbol of America's industrial might, insists that it needs a lower wage tier to remain competitive. "A few people I work with are living at home with their parents," Arnold said. "Some are even on food stamps."

* * *

At a Koch Foods poultry plant in Tennessee, the managers were so intent on keeping the line running all out that Antonia Lopez Paz and the other workers who carved off chicken tenders were ordered not to go to the bathroom except during their lunch and coffee breaks. When one desperate woman asked permission to go, her supervisor took off his hard hat and said, "You can go to the bathroom in this." Some women ended up soiling themselves.

* * *

Don Jensen anticipated a relaxing life of golf after retiring from his human resources post with Lucent Technologies in New Jersey, where he was in charge of recruiting graduates from Stanford, Cornell, MIT, and other top universities. But when Lucent increased its retirees' health insurance premiums to $8,280 a year, up from $180, Jensen was forced to abandon his retirement. He took a job as a ten-dollar-an-hour bank teller.

* * *

As part of her software company's last-lap sprint to get new products out the door, Myra Bronstein sometimes had to work twenty-four hours straight testing for bugs. She felt great loyalty to the Seattle-area company because its executives had repeatedly promised, "As long as we're in business, you have a job." But one Friday morning the company suddenly fired Bronstein and seventeen other quality assurance engineers. The engineers were told that if they wanted to receive severance pay, they had to agree to spend the next month training the workers from India who would be replacing them.

* * *

One of the least examined but most important trends taking place in the United States today is the broad decline in the status and treatment of American workers—white-collar and blue-collar workers, middle-class and low-end workers—that began nearly three decades ago, gradually gathered momentum, and hit with full force soon after the turn of the century. A profound shift has left a broad swath of the American workforce on a lower plane than in decades past, with health coverage, pension benefits, job security, workloads, stress levels, and often wages growing worse for millions of workers.

That the American worker faces this squeeze in the early years of this century is particularly troubling because the squeeze has occurred while the economy, corporate profits, and worker productivity have all been growing robustly. In recent years, a disconcerting disconnect has emerged, with corporate profits soaring while workers' wages stagnated.

The statistical evidence for this squeeze is as compelling as it is disturbing. In 2005, median income for nonelderly households failed to increase for the fifth year in a row, after factoring in for inflation. That is unprecedented in a time of economic growth. In 2006, median income for those households did finally rise, but it still remained lower—$2,375 lower—than six years earlier. That, too, is unprecedented. Even though corporate profits have doubled since recession gave way to economic expansion in November 2001, and even though employee productivity has risen more than 15 percent since then, the average wage for the typical American worker has inched up just 1 percent (after inflation). With the subprime mortgage crisis threatening to pull the economy into recession, some economists say this may be the first time in American history that the typical working household goes through an economic expansion without any increase in income whatsoever.

This, unfortunately, is the continuation of a long-term squeeze. Since 1979, hourly earnings for 80 percent of American workers (those in private-sector, nonsupervisory jobs) have risen by just 1 percent after inflation. The average hourly wage was $17.71 at the end of 2007. For male workers, the average wage has actually slid by 5 percent since 1979. Worker productivity, meanwhile, has climbed 60 percent. If wages had kept pace with productivity, the average full-time worker would be earning $58,000 a year; $36,000 was the average in 2007. The nation's economic pie is growing, but corporations by and large have not given their workers a bigger piece.

The squeeze on the American worker has meant more poverty, more income inequality, more family tensions, more hours at work, more time away from the kids, more families without health insurance, more retirees with inadequate pensions, and more demands on government and taxpayers to provide housing assistance and health coverage. Twenty percent of families with children under six live below the poverty line, and 22 million full-time workers do not have health insurance. Largely as a result of the squeeze, the number of housing foreclosures and personal bankruptcies more than tripled in the quarter century after 1979. Economic studies show that income inequality in the United States is so great that it more closely resembles the inequality of a third world country than that of an advanced industrial nation.

NOTES AND QUESTIONS

1. Greenhouse's book was published in early 2008, before the worst period of the 2008–2009 recession. Therefore, new data about wage stagnation and worker hardships are even more troubling than those he presents. It remains to be seen whether or in what ways the long-term standard of living of the nation's workers will be affected by this latest economic shock. In what ways are workers increasingly vulnerable due to global economic conditions? To what extent does the weak financial situation of many employers affect their treatment of their employees?

2. The conduct of the employers in some of the vignettes in the Greenhouse excerpt is clearly unlawful. For example, it is unlawful to discharge an employee for filing a workers' compensation claim, and it is unlawful to fail to pay employees for time worked "off the clock." In every day life, is the law powerless to protect employees from exploitation by some unscrupulous employers?

3. In an economic downturn should laws (and their enforcement) regulating the workplace be "relaxed" to encourage employers to increase employment or should they be "expanded" to protect workers? Are there historical precedents?

CHAPTER 2

THE DEVELOPMENT OF EMPLOYMENT LAW

B. SOURCES OF MODERN EMPLOYMENT LAW

1. CIVIL SERVICE/PUBLIC EMPLOYMENT

Page 45. Please add the following notes.

4A. For purposes of First Amendment protection, it is important to determine whether an employee is in a policy-making position. Is a deputy property valuation administrator, with responsibility for deed conveyances, tax exonerations, and tax assessments, a policy-making employee? See Murphy v. Cockrell, 505 F.3d 446 (6th Cir. 2007) (held: no; employee's discretionary authority merely involved applying the rules and standards in state statutes).

4B. A county employee in a non-policy-making position was discharged because she refused to campaign for her boss, a county commissioner. The defendant argued that the discharge was lawful because it was not based on the employee's campaigning for an opponent. What result? See Gann v. Cline, 519 F.3d 1090 (10th Cir. 2008) (held: First Amendment protection includes refusal to campaign).

Page 46. Please add the following note.

6. In Fields v. Prater, 566 F.3d 381 (4th Cir. 2009), an unsuccessful applicant for promotion to the position of local director of a county social services department alleged she was not promoted because of her political party affiliation. In holding that political affiliation was an impermissible factor for denial of the promotion, the Fourth Circuit discussed the two-part test used to determine whether the position involved is "policymaking." First is whether the position involves government decisionmaking on issues where there is room for political disagreement on goals or their implementation. Second is whether the responsibility of the position resembles a policymaker, someone privy to confidential information, a communicator, or some other office holder whose function is such that party affiliation is an appropriate requirement.

6. ARBITRATION

Page 64. Please add the following note.

4A. In 14 Penn Plaza LLC v. Pyett, ___ U.S. ___, 129 S.Ct. 1456 (2009), the Supreme Court, 5–4, held that a provision in a collective bargaining agreement that clearly and unmistakably required union members to arbitrate ADEA claims was enforceable as a matter of federal law. The dissenters (Souter, Stevens, Breyer, and Ginsburg) relied on Alexander v. Gardner–Denver Co., 415 U.S. 36 (1974), which held that the Title VII nondiscrimination rights of individuals could not be waived by a union in a collective bargaining agreement. The dissent would apply *Gardner–Denver* to ADEA claims. In addressing this issue, the majority opinion of Justice Thomas reads *Gardner–Denver* more narrowly than the dissent. The arbitrator in *Gardner–Denver* had ruled on the issue of wrongful discharge but did not rule on the issue of discrimination. *"Gardner–Denver* and its progeny thus do not control the outcome where, as is the case here, the collective bargaining agreement's arbitration provision expressly covers both statutory and contractual discrimination claims." 129 S.Ct. at 1469.

4B. In Rent–A–Center, West v. Jackson, 130 S.Ct. 2772 (2010), the Supreme Court held, 5–4, that under the Federal Arbitration Act, where the parties have signed an agreement to arbitrate all future disputes, including the validity of the agreement, the arbitrator and not any court has the authority to determine the enforceability of the agreement.

8. THE "BIG PICTURE"

Page 71. Please add the following note.

3. Despite the plethora of employment legislation enacted in the United States, discussed in the later chapters of this book, many workers are largely excluded from regulatory protections. Among those excluded from coverage are the following: workers for small employers below the statutory minimum number of employees for coverage; workers classified as independent contractors; workers not meeting the definition of employee (e.g., prison labor, participants in welfare-to-work programs, trainees, and students); employees specifically excluded from coverage (e.g., domestic household employees, agricultural workers); and undocumented alien workers. For a further discussion, see Noah Zatz, Working Beyond the Reach or Grasp of Employment Law, in The Gloves–Off Economy: Problems and Possibilities at the Bottom of America's Labor Market (Annette Bernhardt et al. eds. 2008).

PART II

Establishing the Employment Relationship

CHAPTER 3

The Hiring Process

A. Introduction

Page 86. Please add the following to note 7.

See Adamson v. Multi Community Diversified Services, Inc., 514 F.3d 1136 (10th Cir. 2008) (anti-nepotism policy did not violate Title VII).

B. Legal Restrictions on Access to Jobs

1. Undocumented Aliens

Page 109. Please add the following notes before the *Williams* case.

3A. A similar result was reached in Bollinger Shipyards, Inc. v. Director, Office of Worker's Compensation Programs, 604 F.3d 864 (5th Cir. 2010). An undocumented alien, who had falsely stated he was a U.S. citizen and provided a false Social Security number to his employer, was injured while employed as a pipefitter. The Fifth Circuit held that the Longshoremen's and Harbor Workers' Compensation Act (LHWCA) provides that aliens are entitled to compensation and does not differentiate between documented and undocumented aliens. The court distinguished *Hoffman*, noting that under the LHWCA compensation is nondiscretionary and the sole remedy available.

4. In Ramroop v. Flexo–Craft Printing, Inc., 896 N.E.2d 69 (N.Y. 2008), a workers' compensation claimant was denied additional compensation for vocational rehabilitation services because, as an undocumented alien, he could not be legally employed in the United States.

5. In Reyes v. Van Elk, 56 Cal.Rptr.3d 68 (Ct. App. 2007), the plaintiff-employee sued his employer for wages allegedly due under California wage law. The trial court granted summary judgment in favor of the employer based on *Hoffman*. The Court of Appeals reversed, noting that Cal. Lab. Code § 1171.5 expressly provides that immigration status is irrelevant to claims under California's labor, employment, civil rights, and employee housing laws. The court said that allowing employers to hire undocumented workers and pay them less than the wage mandated by the state would create a strong incentive for employers to do so. It also would drive down the wages and working conditions of documented workers. Accord, Coma Corp. v. Kansas Dep't of Labor, 154 P.3d 1080 (Kan. 2007).

6. The Ninth Circuit held that the Legal Arizona Workers Act, imposing sanctions on employers that knowingly hire unauthorized workers and requiring all Arizona employers to use "E–Verify," a voluntary electronic employment verification system administered by the federal government, is not preempted by IRCA. The court said that the statute fell within the savings clause of IRCA's preemption provision and that Congress "could have, but did not, expressly forbid state laws from requiring E–Verify participation." Chicanos Por La Causa, Inc. v. Napolitano, 558 F.3d 856 (9th Cir. 2009), cert. granted sub. nom. Chamber of Commerce of U.S. v. Candelaria, 130 S.Ct. ___ (2010).

2.   RESIDENCY REQUIREMENTS

Page 118.   Please add the following note before part C.

A Note on Veterans Employment, Reemployment, and Preference Laws

A variety of federal and state laws have been enacted to encourage military service by prohibiting discrimination against individuals based on their military service. The Uniformed Services Employment and Reemployment Rights Act of 1994 (USERRA), 38 U.S.C. § 4311, prohibits hiring discrimination against current, past, and potential future service members when military service is a motivating factor in the adverse action. USERRA also requires employers to reinstate individuals who have left their employment to fulfill military obligations. The individual must be reinstated to a position and with seniority equivalent to what he or she would have had if the service had not occurred. The employer need not offer reemployment if it would be unreasonable because of a change in circumstances, it would cause the employer undue hardship, the individual had no reasonable expectation of reemployment, or there was a legally justified reason to discharge the employee before departure for military service.

Veterans also are entitled to hiring preferences under several federal and state laws. The Veterans Preference Act of 1944, 5 U.S.C. §§ 851–869, which gives veterans a preference for federal civil service jobs, has been amended several times and is now codified in various laws regulating the federal civil service, including the Veterans Opportunities Act of 1998, 5 U.S.C. § 3330a. A variety of state laws also provide for veterans preference in state employment. See V.I. Brown, Veterans Preference Employment Statutes: A State-by-State and Federal Government Handbook (2000).

C.   APPLICATIONS, INTERVIEWS, AND REFERENCES

3.   REFERENCES

Page 135.   Please add the following note.

7. In Nelson v. NASA, 530 F.3d 865 (9th Cir. 2008), cert. granted, 130 S.Ct. 1755 (2010), the plaintiffs were scientists, engineers, and administrative personnel at the Jet Propulsion Laboratory. They were employed by the California Institute of Technology and worked as contract employees of NASA. All were deemed "low risk" and none worked with classified material. When NASA imposed a new requirement that all employees were subject to detailed background investigations, including "financial integrity," "mental or emotional stability," and "general behavior or conduct," the employees sued to enjoin the use of such investigations as a condition of employment. The district court denied the injunction, but the Ninth Circuit reversed. It held that the plaintiffs had raised serious questions about the merits of their informational privacy claims. It remanded the case for the district court to fashion a preliminary injunction. The Supreme Court has granted certiorari.

D.   TRUTH-DETECTING DEVICES AND PSYCHOLOGICAL AND PERSONALITY TESTS

1.   THE POLYGRAPH

Page 148.   Please add the following note.

7. For a further discussion, see generally Jon M. Sands, The Lie Detectors: The History of an American Obsession (2008).

2.   Other Truth–Detecting Devices and Psychological and Personality Tests

Page 160.   Please add the following note.

6.   For a further discussion, see Deirdre M. Smith, The Paradox of Personality: Mental Illness, Employment Discrimination, and the Americans with Disabilities Act, 17 Geo. Mason U. Civ. Rts. L.J. 79 (2006).

E.   Medical Screening

2.   Medical Questionnaires

Page 168.   Please add the following at the end of the first paragraph.

Charles Wood, an assistant kiln operator in a cement plant was given a medical examination as part of his application to change his status from part-time to full-time. A chest x-ray indicated a mass in his lung, which required medical attention. At the recommendation of the examining physician, Wood's employment offer was conditioned on his stopping smoking. Wood agreed. He was subsequently discharged when a required urine test was positive for cotinine, the metabolite of nicotine. Wood sued, asserting that his discharge violated a state law prohibiting the discharge of an employee for using tobacco products off the premises during non-working hours. The Supreme Court of South Dakota held that, under the circumstances, the no-smoking restriction placed on the employee was a reasonable bona fide occupational requirement within the meaning of the statute. Wood v. South Dakota Cement Plant, 588 N.W.2d 227 (S.D. 1999). See generally Leslie Zellers, Meliah A. Thomas, & Marice Ashe, Legal Risks to Employers Who Allow Smoking in the Workplace, 97 Am. J. Pub. Health 1376 (2007).

As of July 2010, over half the states have laws requiring that private sector workplaces be smoke free. Some states have special provisions applicable to bars and restaurants.

F.   Drug Testing and Other Laboratory Procedures

1.   Drug Testing

Page 191.   Please add the following note.

6A.   A Department of Transportation (DOT) regulation applies to the drug tests of employees in aviation, rail, motor carrier, and other industries regulated by DOT who are returning to work after successfully completing drug treatment or who failed or refused to take an earlier drug test. As to these individuals, the urine drug tests must be taken using "direct observation" of the specimen production. Does the regulation constitute an unreasonable search and seizure under the Fourth Amendment? See BNSF Ry. Co. v. U.S. Dep't of Transp., 566 F.3d 200 (D.C.Cir. 2009) (held: no violation; safety-sensitive duties of employees in pervasively regulated industry justified the regulation).

Page 191. Please add the following to the end of note 7.

In Williams v. United Parcel Service, 527 F.3d 1135 (10th Cir. 2008), the court held that Oklahoma's drug testing law, which established procedural protections for employee drug testing, did not apply to drug testing subject to regulations imposed by the federal Department of Transportation.

7A. In Lanier v. City of Woodburn, 518 F.3d 1147 (9th Cir. 2008), an applicant challenged a city's policy requiring that all applicants pass a preemployment drug test. The city's main justification was that drug abuse is a serious societal problem. The Ninth Circuit struck down the policy, holding, based on Chandler v. Miller, that a suspicionless drug test not involving a safety-sensitive position or drug interdiction must be based on special needs and may not be merely symbolic.

Page 191. Please add the following to note 8.

In Ross v. RagingWire Telecommunications, Inc., 174 P.3d 200 (Cal. 2008), the California Supreme Court held that firing an employee for failing a drug test for marijuana did not violate the state Compassionate Use Act. The court held that there was no evidence that the statute was intended to apply in the workplace.

Page 194. Please add the following to the NOTE.

According to a 2007 study by the Substance Abuse and Mental Health Services Administration, about 8.2% of full-time workers admitted to using illicit drugs over the past month, including marijuana, cocaine, heroin, hallucinogens, inhalants, or prescriptive psychotherapeutics used non-medicinally. The most common substance of abuse was marijuana. The occupations reporting the highest usage were food service (17.4%) and construction (15.1%). Among the lowest were teachers (4.0%), social service workers (4.0%), and protective service workers (3.4%).

2. GENETIC DISCRIMINATION

Page 202. Please insert the following before "3."

GENETIC INFORMATION NONDISCRIMINATION ACT OF 2008 (GINA), P.L. 110–233, 122 Stat. 881 (2008)

[relevant portions of this law appear in the Appendix at the end of this supplement]

Title II of GINA prohibits employers, employment agencies, and labor organizations from requiring or requesting that an individual undergo a genetic test as a condition of employment. It also prohibits discrimination on the basis of "genetic information," defined as information about an individual's genetic tests, the genetic tests of family members, or the occurrence of a disease in family members of the individual.

For private sector employers, GINA has the same coverage and remedies as Title VII, except that disparate impact claims may not be brought. The employment provisions of GINA take effect 18 months after enactment (November 21, 2009). The EEOC's proposed regulations [on] GINA appear at 74 Fed. Reg. 9056 (2009).

Mark A. Rothstein, GINA, the ADA, and Genetic Discrimination in Employment

36 J.L. Med. & Ethics 837 (2008).

The Genetic Information Nondiscrimination Act of 2008 (GINA) was signed into law on May 21, 2008, after a 13–year struggle in Congress. GINA prohibits genetic discrimination in employment and health insurance, thereby supplementing existing federal protections against genetic discrimination in employer-sponsored group health plans contained in the federal Health Insurance Portability and Accountability Act of 1996 (HIPAA) and state laws prohibiting genetic discrimination in employment and individual health insurance.

Although there have been very few documented instances of genetic discrimination in health insurance and employment, the fear of such discrimination has led many at-risk individuals to decline genetic testing in both the clinical and research settings. The findings section of GINA specifically states that federal legislation "is necessary to fully protect the public from discrimination and allay their concerns about the potential for discrimination, thereby allowing individuals to take advantage of genetic testing, technologies, research, and new therapies."

The approach and relative merits of GINA are subject to debate, but even its supporters recognize that GINA has major shortcomings. Three of the most commonly noted deficiencies are the following.

First, GINA's ban on genetic discrimination is not comprehensive. GINA does not apply to life insurance, disability insurance, long-term care insurance, or other potential uses of genetic information. Consequently, it is not clear that its limited protections will be sufficient to allay the fears of individuals currently dissuaded from undergoing genetic testing.

Second, GINA prohibits discrimination based on genotype, but not phenotype. Thus, GINA only applies to individuals who are asymptomatic. In the health insurance context, individuals are protected from discrimination based on their genetic risk of disease, but they are not protected if they develop the disease. In the overwhelming number of states, health insurance companies may lawfully raise the rates or refuse to renew the policies of individuals based on a change in their health condition. [Note: Health reform legislation enacted in 2010 eliminated this concern. See Chapter 6.]

Third, the employment provisions of GINA prohibit employers from requiring or requesting an individual to undergo genetic testing or disclosing the results of a genetic test as a condition of employment. Nevertheless, GINA does not affect a key provision of the Americans with Disabilities Act (ADA), under which an employer may, after a conditional offer of employment, lawfully require an individual to sign an authorization to disclose all of his or her health records to the employer. Because there is currently no feasible way to segregate genetic from non-genetic information in either paper or electronic health records, it must be anticipated that, notwithstanding GINA, many—if not most—custodians of health records will continue the practice of sending requesting employers all of an individual's health records upon receipt of an authorization.

NOTES AND QUESTIONS

1. What is the relationship between the coverage of GINA and the ADA? Are there any gaps in coverage?

2. On August 30, 2009, the Board of Trustees of the University of Akron adopted a new policy that, in addition to criminal background checks, "at discretion of the University of Akron, any applicant may be asked to submit fingerprints or DNA sample for purpose of a federal criminal background check." The policy, expressly prohibited by GINA, created a substantial amount of adverse publicity, and was repealed by the university on November 5, 2009. Coincidentally, GINA became effective on November 21, 2009. See Declan McCullagh, University Backs Away From New–Hire DNA Testing (Nov. 6, 2009) www.cbsnews.com/sections/taking_liberties/main 504383.shtml?contributor45134. For a further discussion, see Shawneequa L. Callier, John Huss, & Eric T. Juengst, GINA and Preemployment Criminal Background Checks, 40 Hastings Center Rep. No. 1 at 15 (Jan.-Feb. 2010).

3. For a further discussion of GINA, see Jessica Roberts, Preempting Discrimination: Lessons from the Genetic Information Nondiscrimination Act, 63 Vand. L. Rev. 439 (2010).

G.   NEGLIGENT HIRING

Page 209.   Please add the following notes.

4A. Hawaii, New York, Pennsylvania, and Wisconsin have laws prohibiting discrimination in employment on the basis of a criminal conviction. All of the laws have exceptions if the conviction relates to the job. See generally Jonathan J. Darrow, Adverse Employment Consequences Triggered by Criminal Convictions: Recent Cases Interpret State Statutes Prohibiting Discrimination, 42 Wake Forest L. Rev. 991 (2007).

5. See El v. SEPTA, 479 F.3d 232 (3d Cir. 2007) (upholding employer's business necessity defense for refusal to hire on the basis of a criminal conviction).

Page 211. Please delete the *Richland* case and replace it with the following.

Kadlec Medical Center v. Lakeview Anesthesia Associates

527 F.3d 412 (5th Cir. 2008).

■ REAVLEY, CIRCUIT JUDGE:

Kadlec Medical Center and its insurer, Western Professional Insurance Company, filed this diversity action in Louisiana district court against Louisiana Anesthesia Associates (LAA), its shareholders, and Lakeview Regional Medical Center (Lakeview Medical). The LAA shareholders worked with Dr. Robert Berry—an anesthesiologist and former LAA shareholder—at Lakeview Medical, where the defendants discovered his on-duty use of narcotics. In referral letters written by the defendants and relied on by Kadlec, his future employer, the defendants did not disclose Dr. Berry's drug use.

While under the influence of Demerol at Kadlec, Dr. Berry's negligent performance led to the near-death of a patient, resulting in a lawsuit against Kadlec. Plaintiffs claim here that the defendants' misleading referral letters were a legal cause of plaintiffs' financial injury, i.e., having to pay over $8 million to defend and settle the lawsuit. The jury found in favor of the plaintiffs and judgment followed. We reverse the judgment against Lakeview Medical, vacate the remainder of the judgment, and remand.

I. Factual Background

Dr. Berry was a licensed anesthesiologist in Louisiana and practiced with Drs. William Preau, Mark Dennis, David Baldone, and Allan Parr at LAA. From November 2000 until his termination on March 13, 2001, Dr. Berry was a shareholder of LAA, the exclusive provider of anesthesia services to Lakeview Medical (a Louisiana hospital).

In November 2000, a small management team at Lakeview Medical investigated Dr. Berry after nurses expressed concern about his undocumented and suspicious withdrawals of Demerol. The investigative team found excessive Demerol withdrawals by Dr. Berry and a lack of documentation for the withdrawals.

Lakeview Medical CEO Max Lauderdale discussed the team's findings with Dr. Berry and Dr. Dennis. Dr. Dennis then discussed Dr. Berry's situation with his partners. They all agreed that Dr. Berry's use of Demerol had to be controlled and monitored. But Dr. Berry did not follow the agreement or account for his continued Demerol withdrawals. Three months later, Dr. Berry failed to answer a page while on-duty at Lakeview Medical. He was discovered in the call-room, asleep, groggy, and unfit to work. Personnel immediately called Dr. Dennis, who found Dr. Berry not communicating well and unable to work. Dr. Dennis had Dr. Berry taken away after Dr. Berry said that he had taken prescription medications.

Lauderdale, Lakeview Medical's CEO, decided that it was in the best interest of patient safety that Dr. Berry not practice at the hospital. Dr. Dennis and his three partners at LAA fired Dr. Berry and signed his termination letter on March 27, 2001, which explained that he was fired "for cause":

> [You have been fired for cause because] you have reported to work in an impaired physical, mental, and emotional state. Your impaired condition has prevented you from properly performing your duties and puts our patients at significant risk.... [P]lease consider your termination effective March 13, 2001.

At Lakeview Medical, Lauderdale ordered the Chief Nursing Officer to notify the administration if Dr. Berry returned.

Despite recognizing Dr. Berry's drug problem and the danger he posed to patients, neither Dr. Dennis nor Lauderdale reported Dr. Berry's impairment to the hospital's Medical Executive Committee, eventually noting only that Dr. Berry was "no longer employed by LAA." Neither one reported Dr. Berry's impairment to Lakeview Medical's Board of Trustees, and no one on behalf of Lakeview Medical reported Dr. Berry's impairment or discipline to the Louisiana Board of Medical Examiners or to the National Practitioner's Data Bank. In fact, at some point Lauderdale took the unusual step of locking away in his office all files, audits, plans, and notes concerning Dr. Berry and the investigation.

After leaving LAA and Lakeview Medical, Dr. Berry briefly obtained work as a *locum tenens* (traveling physician) at a hospital in Shreveport, Louisiana. In October 2001, he applied through Staff Care, a leading *locum tenens* staffing firm, for *locum tenens* privileges at Kadlec Medical Center in Washington State. After receiving his application, Kadlec began its credentialing process. Kadlec examined a variety of materials, including referral letters from LAA and Lakeview Medical.

LAA's Dr. Preau and Dr. Dennis, two months after firing Dr. Berry for his on-the-job drug use, submitted referral letters for Dr. Berry to Staff Care, with the intention that they be provided to future employers. The letter from Dr. Dennis stated that he had worked with Dr. Berry for four years, that he was an excellent clinician, and that he would be an asset to any anesthesia service. Dr. Preau's letter said that he worked with Berry at Lakeview Medical and that he recommended him highly as an anesthesiologist. Dr. Preau's and Dr. Dennis's letters were submitted on June 3, 2001, only sixty-eight days after they fired him for using narcotics while on-duty and stating in his termination letter that Dr. Berry's behavior put "patients at significant risk."

On October 17, 2001, Kadlec sent Lakeview Medical a request for credentialing information about Berry. The request included a detailed confidential questionnaire, a delineation of privileges, and a signed consent for release of information. The interrogatories on the questionnaire asked whether "[Dr. Berry] has been subject to any disciplinary action," if "[Dr. Berry has] the ability (health status) to perform the privileges requested," whether "[Dr. Berry has] shown any signs of behavior/personality problems or impairments," and whether Dr. Berry has satisfactory "judgment."

Nine days later, Lakeview Medical responded to the requests for credentialing information about fourteen different physicians. In thirteen cases, it responded fully and completely to the request, filling out forms with all the information asked for by the requesting health care provider. The fourteenth request, from Kadlec concerning Berry, was handled differently. Instead of completing the multi-part forms, Lakeview Medical staff drafted a short letter. In its entirety, it read:

> This letter is written in response to your inquiry regarding [Dr. Berry]. Due to the large volume of inquiries received in this office, the following information is provided.

> Our records indicate that Dr. Robert L. Berry was on the Active Medical Staff of Lakeview Regional Medical Center in the field of Anesthesiology from March 04, 1997 through September 04, 2001.

> If I can be of further assistance, you may contact me at (504) 867–4076.

* * *

Kadlec then credentialed Dr. Berry, and he began working there. After working at Kadlec without incident for a number of months, he moved temporarily to Montana where he worked at Benefis Hospital. During his stay in Montana, he was in a car accident and suffered a back injury. Kadlec's head of anesthesiology and the credentialing department all knew of Dr. Berry's accident and back injury, but they did not investigate whether it would impair his work.

After Dr. Berry returned to Kadlec, some nurses thought that he appeared sick and exhibited mood swings. One nurse thought that Dr. Berry's entire demeanor had changed and that he should be watched closely. In mid-September 2002, Dr. Berry gave a patient too much morphine during surgery, and she had to be revived using Narcan. The neurosurgeon was irate about the incident.

On November 12, 2002, Dr. Berry was assigned to the operating room beginning at 6:30 a.m. He worked with three different surgeons and multiple nurses well into the afternoon. According to one nurse, Dr. Berry was "screwing up all day" and several of his patients suffered adverse affects from not being properly anesthetized. He had a hacking cough and multiple nurses thought he looked sick. During one procedure, he apparently almost passed out.

Kimberley Jones was Dr. Berry's fifth patient that morning. She was in for what should have been a routine, fifteen minute tubal ligation. When they moved her into the recovery room, one nurse noticed that her fingernails were blue, and she was not breathing. Dr. Berry failed to resuscitate her, and she is now in a permanent vegetative state.

Dr. Berry's nurse went directly to her supervisor the next morning and expressed concern that Dr. Berry had a narcotics problem. Dr. Berry later admitted to Kadlec staff that he had been diverting and using Demerol since his June car accident in Montana and that he had become addicted to Demerol. Dr. Berry wrote a confession, and he immediately admitted himself into a drug rehabilitation program.

Jones's family sued Dr. Berry and Kadlec in Washington. Dr. Berry's insurer settled the claim against him. After the Washington court ruled that Kadlec would be responsible for Dr. Berry's conduct under respondeat superior, Western, Kadlec's insurer, settled the claim against Kadlec.

II. Procedural History

* * *

Plaintiffs' surviving claims for intentional and negligent misrepresentation arise out of the alleged misrepresentations in, and omissions from, the defendants' referral letters for Dr. Berry. These claims were tried to a jury, which returned a verdict in favor of the plaintiffs on both claims. The jury awarded plaintiffs $8.24 million, which is approximately equivalent to the amount Western spent settling the Jones lawsuit ($7.5 million) plus the amount it spent on attorneys fees, costs, and expenses (approximately $744,000) associated with the Jones lawsuit.

* * *

III. Discussion

A. The Intentional and Negligent Misrepresentation Claims

The plaintiffs allege that the defendants committed two torts: intentional misrepresentation and negligent misrepresentation. The elements of a claim for *intentional* misrepresentation in Louisiana are: (1) a misrepresentation of a material fact; (2) made with intent to deceive; and (3) causing justifiable reliance with resultant injury. To establish a claim for intentional misrepresentation when it is by silence or inaction, plaintiffs also must show that the defendant owed a duty to the plaintiff to disclose the information. To make out a *negligent* misrepresentation claim in Louisiana: (1) there must be a legal duty on the part of the defendant to supply correct information; (2) there must be a breach of that duty, which can occur by omission as well as by affirmative misrepresentation; and (3) the breach must have caused damages to the plaintiff based on the plaintiff's reasonable reliance on the misrepresentation.

* * *

1. *The Affirmative Misrepresentations*

The defendants owed a duty to Kadlec to avoid affirmative misrepresentations in the referral letters. In Louisiana, "[a]lthough a party may keep absolute silence and violate no rule of law or equity, ... if he volunteers to speak and to convey information which may influence the conduct of the other party, he is bound to [disclose] the whole truth." In negligent misrepresentation cases, Louisiana courts have held that even when there is no initial duty to disclose information, "once [a party] volunteer[s] information, it assume[s] a duty to insure that the information volunteered [is] correct."

Consistent with these cases, the defendants had a legal duty not to make affirmative misrepresentations in their referral letters. A party does not incur liability every time it casually makes an incorrect statement. But if an employer makes a misleading statement in a referral letter about the performance of its former employee, the former employer may be liable for its statements if the facts and circumstances warrant. Here, defendants were recommending an anesthesiologist, who held the lives of patients in his hands every day. Policy considerations dictate that the defendants had a duty to avoid misrepresentations in their referral letters if they misled plaintiffs into thinking that Dr. Berry was an "excellent" anesthesiologist, when they had information that he was a drug addict. Indeed, if defendants' statements created a misapprehension about Dr. Berry's suitability to work as an anesthesiologist, then by "volunteer[ing] to speak and to convey information which ... influence[d] the conduct of [Kadlec], [they were] bound to [disclose] the whole truth." In other words, if they created a misapprehension about Dr. Berry due to their own statements, they incurred a duty to disclose information about his drug use and for-cause firing to complete the whole picture.

We now review whether there is evidence that the defendants' letters were misleading. We start with the LAA defendants. The letter from Dr. Preau stated that Dr. Berry was an "excellent anesthesiologist" and that he "recommend[ed] him highly." Dr. Dennis's letter said that Dr. Berry was "an excellent physician" who "he is sure will be an asset to [his future employer's] anesthesia service." These letters are false on their face and materially misleading. Notably, these letters came only sixty-eight days after Drs. Dennis and Preau, on behalf of LAA, signed a letter terminating Dr. Berry for using narcotics while on-duty and stating that Dr. Berry's behavior put "patients at significant risk." Furthermore, because of the misleading statements in the letters, Dr. Dennis and Dr. Preau incurred a duty to cure these misleading statements by disclosing to Kadlec that Dr. Berry had been fired for on-the-job drug use.

The question as to whether Lakeview Medical's letter was misleading is more difficult. The letter does not comment on Dr. Berry's proficiency as an anesthesiologist, and it does not recommend him to Kadlec. Kadlec says that the letter is misleading because Lakeview Medical stated that it could not reply to Kadlec's detailed inquiry in full "[d]ue to the large volume of inquiries received." But whatever the real reason that Lakeview Medical did not respond in full to Kadlec's inquiry, Kadlec did not present evidence that this could have affirmatively misled it into thinking that Dr. Berry had an uncheckered history at Lakeview Medical.

* * *

In sum, we hold that the letters from the LAA defendants were affirmatively misleading, but the letter from Lakeview Medical was not. Therefore, Lakeview Medical cannot be held liable based on its alleged affirmative misrepresentations. It can only be liable if it had an affirmative duty to disclose information about Dr. Berry. We now examine the theory that, even assuming that there were no misleading statements in the referral letters, the defendants had an affirmative duty to disclose. We discuss this theory with regard to both defendants for reasons that will be clear by the end of the opinion.

2. *The Duty to Disclose*

In Louisiana, a duty to disclose does not exist absent special circumstances, such as a fiduciary or confidential relationship between the parties, which, under the circumstances, justifies the imposition of the duty. Louisiana cases suggest that before a duty to disclose is imposed the defendant must have had a pecuniary interest in the transaction. In Louisiana, the existence of a duty is a question of law, and we review the duty issue here *de novo.*

* * *

Plaintiffs argue that policy considerations weigh in favor of recognizing a duty to disclose. They contend that imposing a duty on health care employers to disclose that a physician's drug dependence could pose a serious threat to patient safety promotes important policy goals recognized by Louisiana courts. The Louisiana legislature recently adopted legislation that requires health care entities to "report [to the appropriate professional licensing board] each instance in which the health care entity ... [t]akes an adverse action against a health care professional due to impairment or possible impairment.'' This shows that the legislature has recognized the importance of reporting possible impairments that could affect patient safety.

Despite these compelling policy arguments, we do not predict that courts in Louisiana—absent misleading statements such as those made by the LAA defendants—would impose an affirmative duty to disclose. The defendants did not have a fiduciary or contractual duty to disclose what it knew to Kadlec. And although the defendants might have had an ethical obligation to disclose their knowledge of Dr. Berry's drug problems, they were also rightly concerned about a possible defamation claim if they communicated negative information about Dr. Berry. As a general policy matter, even if an employer believes that its disclosure is protected because of the truth of the matter communicated, it would be burdensome to impose a duty on employers, upon receipt of a employment referral request, to investigate whether the negative information it has about an employee fits within the courts' description of *which* negative information must be disclosed to the future employer. Finally, concerns about protecting employee privacy weigh in favor of not mandating a potentially broad duty to disclose.

NOTES AND QUESTIONS

1. From the perspective of Kimberly Jones and her family, is there a moral difference between the deliberate omission of Lakeview Medical Center and the deliberate commissions of the physicians of Louisiana Anesthesia Associates? Should the law recognize a distinction?

2. Why do you think the defendants were unwilling to write a truthful letter of recommendation or file a report of Dr. Berry's drug problem?

3. The American Medical Association's Code of Medical Ethics provides in part: "A physician shall uphold the standards of professionalism, be honest in all professional interactions, and strive to report physicians deficient in character or competence, or engaging in fraud or deception, to appropriate entities." American Medical Association, Code of Medical Ethics 2006–2007 ed., Preamble § II (2006). Section 9.031 also requires the reporting of impaired, incompetent, or unethical colleagues. Do you think the anesthesiologists should be sanctioned for writing the letters of recommendation or failing to report Dr. Berry to the state medical licensing board?

4. A grade school student in the Urbana School District was sexually assaulted by a teacher. The teacher previously taught in the McLean School District, where he also had assaulted students. The student sued the McLean School District alleging that officials knew of the assaults, did not report them, and allowed the teacher to resign and get another job at Urbana. The Seventh Circuit held, among other things, that the plaintiff did not state a claim under Illinois tort law for the following reasons: (1) there was no general duty to act affirmatively to protect another from criminal attack by a third party; (2) the state child abuse reporting statute did not create a duty to the abused child when a person fails to file a report; (3) the McLean officials had no special relationship with the victim; and (4) even though the risk may have been foreseeable, it did not create a duty to act. Doe-2 v. McLean County Unit Dist. No. 5 Bd. of Directors, 593 F.3d 507 (7th Cir. 2010).

CHAPTER 4

DISCRIMINATION

A. DISCRIMINATION ON THE BASIS OF RACE OR SEX

1. SOURCES OF PROTECTION

Page 225. Please add the following paragraph before "e. EXECUTIVE ORDER 11246."

Does the Equal Protection Clause provide a cause of action to a government employee who says that his or her dismissal was for arbitrary, vindictive, or malicious reasons? The plaintiff would not be asserting that the mistreatment was because of membership in a group such as race, gender, or age. These claims are therefore denominated "class-of-one"— that the employee was intentionally treated differently from others similarly situated and thus there was no rational basis for the action. Some circuits allowed these actions. The Supreme Court said no—that government, like private employers, can live in an employment-at-will world and discharge for reasons that may appear arbitrary. Chief Justice Roberts said that government as regulator must satisfy a constitutional standard of rationality but that government as employer has greater discretion unless, as with civil service, collective bargaining, or individual contracts, it chooses to grant greater security of employment. Engquist v. Oregon Dep't of Agriculture, 553 U.S. 591 (2008) (6–3).

2. WHAT IS UNLAWFUL DISCRIMINATION?

Page 231. Please delete note 3 and replace with the following note.

3. Has a plaintiff shown pretext where an unbiased decision was made in reliance on information or recommendations provided by a biased subordinate? Most circuits say yes, relying on the "cat's paw" or "rubber stamp" doctrine. Courts are divided as to the level of control a biased subordinate must exert over the employment decision before the employer becomes liable for discrimination. See EEOC v. BCI Coca–Cola Bottling Co. of Los Angeles, 450 F.3d 476 (10th Cir. 2006), cert. dismissed, 549 U.S. 1105 (2007) (holding that termination decision based solely on supervisor's report that was motivated by bias may establish pretext). See also Poland v. Chertoff, 494 F.3d 1174 (9th Cir. 2007) (analyzing circuit split and formulating a new standard).

Page 232.   Please add the following notes.

6.   A plaintiff can establish a prima facie case of gender discrimination simply by showing she was replaced by a man, regardless of their comparative qualifications; she need not show that they were similarly situated. See Vincent v. Brewer, 514 F.3d 489 (6th Cir. 2007).

7.   A white assistant basketball coach at Iona College was terminated after coaching the team to a losing record three years in a row. The coach sued the college under Title VII claiming that he was fired because of his marriage to an African American woman. The relevant clause in Title VII states that it is an "unlawful employment practice for an employer ... to discharge any individual ... because of such individual's race." 42 U.S.C. § 2000e–2(a)(1). Does this language prohibit an employer from discriminating against an employee on the basis of an interracial marriage? See Holcomb v. Iona College, 521 F.3d 130 (2d Cir. 2008) (held: yes).

Page 243.   Please add the following note.

8A.   The judicial decision in *Price Waterhouse* was to some degree overturned in Gross v. FBL Financial Services, Inc., ___ U.S. ___, 129 S.Ct. 2343 (2009). Chief Justice Roberts and Justice Alito, who were not on the Court at the time of *Price Waterhouse*, joined an opinion by Justice Thomas that refused to apply the mixed motive analysis in *Price Waterhouse* to the Age Discrimination in Employment Act, even though the relevant ADEA language is the same as the Title VII language interpreted in *Price Waterhouse*. However, Title VII law continues to encourage mixed motive causes of action because of congressional approval in the 1991 Civil Rights Act, a statute that did not address the ADEA.

Page 244.   Please add the following note.

IMPLICIT BIAS

In recent years, antidiscrimination law scholars have written extensively about the theory of "implicit," or unconscious, bias. Professors Christine Jolls and Cass Sunstein explain that the theory is rooted in cognitive psychology research:

> Much evidence of these forms of implicit bias comes from the Implicit Association Test (IAT), which has been taken by large and diverse populations on the Internet and elsewhere. The IAT asks individuals to perform the seemingly straightforward task of categorizing a series of words or pictures into groups. Two of the groups are racial or other

categories, such as "black" and "white," and two of the groups are the categories "pleasant" and "unpleasant." ... The IAT is rooted in the very simple hypothesis that people will find it easier to associate pleasant words with white faces and names than with African–American faces and names—and that the same pattern will be found for other traditionally disadvantaged groups.

In fact, implicit bias as measured by the IAT has proven to be extremely widespread. Most people tend to prefer white to African–American, young to old, and heterosexual to gay. Strikingly, members of traditionally disadvantaged groups tend to show the same set of preferences.

It might not be so disturbing to find implicit bias in experimental settings if the results did not predict actual behavior, and in fact the relationship between IAT scores and behavior remains an active area of research.... For example, there is strong evidence that scores on the IAT and similar tests are correlated with third parties' ratings of the degree of general friendliness individuals show to members of another race. More particularly, "larger IAT effect scores predicted greater speaking time, more smiling, [and] more extemporaneous social comments" in interactions with whites as compared to African–Americans. And it is reasonable to speculate that such uneasy interactions are associated with biased behavior. In the employment context in particular, even informal differences in treatment may have significant effects on employment outcomes, particularly in today's fluid workplaces. If this is so, then the importance to legal policy is clear. If people are treated differently, and worse, because of their race or another protected trait, then the principle of antidiscrimination has been violated, even if the source of the differential treatment is implicit rather than conscious bias.

Christine Jolls & Cass R. Sunstein, The Law of Implicit Bias, 94 Cal. L. Rev. 969 (2006).

Research in cognitive psychology has shown that IAT bias scores are not fixed; in fact, they appear to be quite malleable. In one study, individuals exhibited decreased levels of bias against African Americans after being shown a photograph of Tiger Woods. See Nilankana Dasgupta & Anthony G. Greenwald, On the Malleability of Automatic Attitudes: Combating Automatic Prejudice with Images of Admired and Disliked Individuals, 81 J. Personality & Soc. Psychol. 800, 803–04 (2001). These lower bias levels remained unchanged twenty-four hours later when the same subjects underwent a second test. In another study, subjects had lower IAT bias scores when an African–American administered the test. See Brian S. Lowery, Curtis D. Hardin & Stacey Sinclair, Social Influence Effects on Automatic Racial Prejudice, 81 J. Personality & Soc. Psychol. 842, 844–45, 846–47 (2001). These results beg an obvious question: if levels of implicit bias are affected by current social and political environments, does the government have a duty to alter those environments and "de-bias" its citizens? Should we instead leave it to culture and the media to shift our unconscious biases? Is there a way in which "de-biasing" would amount to governmental thought control? Does the malleability of implicit bias provide a new defense for affirmative action? See Jerry Kang & Mahzarin R. Banaji, Fair Measures: A Behavioral Realist Revision of "Affirmative Action," 97 Cal. L. Rev. 1063 (2006).

Critics of the significance of implicit bias, however, worry that judges and legislators might heed political calls to reform the law without realizing that they stand on shaky scientific ground. Professors Gregory Mitchell and Philip E. Tetlock argue that using questionable research findings to fashion legal rules could lead to untoward results:

> Our fear is that the stage has been set for an epistemic disaster of minor-epic proportions. Throughout this Article, we have seen how rarely IAT researchers temper their enthusiasm for ferreting out unconscious prejudice with offsetting concerns about the dangers of making false accusations of prejudice.... If the knowledge claims of IAT advocates are as exaggerated as we maintain, IAT advocates are already causing substantial harm to American society by: (a) stimulating excessive suspicion of Whites among Blacks, suspicion that can crystallize into conspiracy theories that poison race relations; (b) convincing Blacks that they are held in contempt, thereby inducing "stereotype threat" and "social-identity threat" that, respectively, increase the likelihood of self-fulfilling prophecies in which Blacks act in ways that confirm the ill opinions they imagine others hold and heighten preconscious attention to subtle cues that confirm the devalued role of minority groups; (c) providing authoritative-sounding but false feedback to a million-plus visitors to IAT websites that they are prejudiced; and (d) providing authoritative-sounding but false grounds for commonality-of-cause requirements in class action litigation.

Gregory Mitchell & Philip E. Tetlock, Antidiscrimination Law and the Perils of Mindreading, 67 Ohio St. L.J. 1023 (2006).

Should lawmakers and judges hesitate to fashion legal rules on the basis of social science research? Professors Linda Krieger and Susan Fiske note that our legal system values predictability and the principle of stare decisis, whereas the social sciences are more welcoming of innovation, revision, and creativity. See Linda Hamilton Krieger & Susan T. Fiske, Behavioral Realism in Employment Discrimination Law: Implicit Bias and Disparate Treatment, 97 Cal. L. Rev. 997 (2006). How can we reconcile these conflicting impulses? In the natural sciences, a hypothesis does not become a "law" until many successful experiments have been completed over a long period of time. Should we apply the same rigorous test to conclusions drawn from social science before permitting them to modify legal doctrines? Is it possible to develop a jurisprudential model for incorporating social scientific research into legal construction and interpretation?

Does the influence of a social science such as economics on the law suggest that we already have developed such a model?

Page 247.   Please add the following note.

5.   In Miller v. Department of Corrections, 115 P.3d 77 (Cal. 2005), a prison warden demonstrated favoritism towards three female employees with whom he had previously had sexual affairs. The California Supreme Court held that "when such sexual favoritism in a workplace is sufficiently widespread it may create an actionable hostile work environment in which the demeaning message is conveyed to female employees that they are viewed by management as 'sexual playthings' or that the way required for women to get ahead is to engage in sexual conduct with their supervisors. . . ."

Page 254.   Please add the following notes.

5.   Some sociological studies support the proposition that mothers are at a severe disadvantage in the job market when compared with other female job applicants. One Cornell study found that employers consistently viewed mothers as less competent or committed and held them to higher standards of performance and punctuality than nonmothers. On average, mothers were 80 percent less likely to be hired and were offered a starting salary $11,000 lower than nonmothers, while fathers were offered the highest salaries of all. Eyal Press, Family–Leave Values, N.Y. Times, July 29, 2007 (citing study by Shelley Correll published in American Journal of Sociology).

6.   The EEOC officially recognized a "connection between parenthood, especially motherhood, and employment discrimination" when it issued an enforcement guidance titled Unlawful Disparate Treatment of Workers with Caregiving Responsibilities in 2007. "An employer may violate Title VII when it takes actions or limits opportunities for employees because of beliefs that the employer has about mothers and caretakers that are linked to sex," said EEOC Commissioner Stuart J. Ishimaru. The enforcement guidance is available at www.eeoc.gov/policy/docs/caregiving.html.

Page 255.   Please add the following sentence to note 2.

Cf. Lulaj v. Wackenhut Corp., 512 F.3d 760 (6th Cir. 2008) (plaintiff made out prima facie case of discrimination where she was promised a promotion to supervisor but was offered a lesser promotion after her employer learned she was pregnant).

Page 256.   Please add the following notes.

7.   What, if any, rights should men have under the PDA? A farm owned by an order of Catholic nuns fired two employees on the same day, a man and his girlfriend, who had become pregnant and suffered two miscarriages while working on the farm. The employer claimed that it terminated the male employee because of dissatisfaction with the way he ran the farm's internship program and the female employee because her services were no longer needed. However, the director of the farm had also expressed concerns about the employees' openness with their relationship and their "behavior contrary to Roman Catholic teachings." The employees, acting pro se, argued that the employer's explanations were pretextual and that the PDA protects males and females equally for "exercising their reproductive rights." The Seventh Circuit disagreed, upholding summary judgment for the employer. Although the PDA's language and purpose speak to discrimination against women, men can still be successful PDA plaintiffs, but their claims must allege discrimination because of sex. Griffin v. Sisters of St. Francis, 489 F.3d 838 (7th Cir. 2007). For a discussion of the PDA and discrimination in benefits, see ch. 6.

8. The PDA says that "because of sex" includes "pregnancy, childbirth, or related medical conditions." The EEOC guidelines say: "A woman is therefore protected against such practices as being fired . . . merely because she is pregnant or has had an abortion." See, e.g., Doe v. C.A.R.S. Protection Plus, Inc., 527 F.3d 358 (3d Cir. 2008).

9. Before enactment of the PDA in 1978, discrimination on the basis of pregnancy was not a violation of Title VII. At that time, AT & T's pension system gave less retirement credit for pregnancy leave than for medical leave generally. After the PDA took effect in 1979, the company equalized treatment of pregnancy leave. The Supreme Court decided in 2009 that the PDA did not apply retroactively, so current pensions affected by the pre–1979 discrimination do not violate Title VII. Justices Ginsburg and Breyer dissented. AT & T Corp. v. Hulteen, __ U.S. __, 129 S.Ct. 1962 (2009).

10. Cheryl Hall said she was fired for taking time off from work to undergo in vitro fertilization. The district court dismissed a Pregnancy Discrimination Act claim, saying infertility is a gender-neutral condition. The court of appeals reversed. The procedure Hall underwent is performed only on women. "Hall was terminated not for the gender-neutral condition of infertility, but rather for the gender-specific quality of childbearing capacity." Hall v. Nalco Co., 534 F.3d 644 (7th Cir. 2008).

Page 262. Please add the following note.

12. What are the costs of antidiscrimination law? Who bears the burden? Professor Christine Jolls argues that many of the costs associated with disparate impact liability are in fact accommodation costs.

> Employers are often required by disparate impact law to incur special costs in response to the distinctive needs or circumstances (measured against existing market structures) of particular groups, and these requirements may arise in situations in which the employer had no intention of treating the group differently on the basis of group membership. Thus, important aspects of disparate impact law are in fact accommodation requirements.

As one example, Professor Jolls argues that when employers are forbidden to use job selection criteria, they are effectively forced to accommodate certain applicants. In Lanning v. Southeastern Pennsylvania Transp. Auth., 181 F.3d 478 (3d Cir. 1999), cert. denied, 528 U.S. 1131 (2000), female plaintiffs challenged a requirement that applicants to the transit police force run 1.5 miles in twelve minutes under a disparate impact theory. The employer responded that there was a business necessity to use the test because it accurately measured aerobic ability, which the employer further demonstrated correlates well to arrests. The Third Circuit reversed a lower court judgment for the employer and held that the test might not constitute a business necessity. Professor Jolls makes the point that, if the test is invalidated on remand, the court will have imposed on the employer the costs of finding an equally effective test that does not have a disparate impact on female applicants. In other words, if the employer adopted this requirement with no intention to discriminate against women, the court is in some ways ordering the employer to accommodate female applicants.

Under the Americans with Disabilities Act, employers must extend reasonable accommodations to individuals with disabilities. The costs of accommodation are borne by the individual employer and will be equitably shared by all employees, both disabled and nondisabled. In the context of disparate impact law, however, Professor Jolls argues that sometimes these costs will be imposed upon precisely those whom the antidiscrimination laws mean to protect.

> The result I wish to highlight here involves the case in which limits on both wage and employment differentials are fully binding on employers. In this case, antidiscrimination law's restrictions on differential job conditions—like requirements of accommodation—ordinarily will make disadvantaged employees better off because the costs of the intervention will be partially shifted to nondisadvantaged employees. This outcome, of course, is not surprising and is presumably the point of the intervention. However, the interesting result I wish to emphasize here is that in certain cases the restrictions on differential job conditions imposed by antidiscrimination law will actually make disadvantaged employees worse off, even though limits on wage and employment differentials between disadvantaged and nondisadvantaged groups are fully binding. This will occur if the disadvantaged group comprises a large fraction of the relevant labor pool and the cost of the legal intervention to employers exceeds its value to disadvantaged employees by a sufficient margin. The intuition here is that if the disadvantaged group comprises a large fraction of the relevant labor pool, then there is not a large group of nondisadvantaged employees to help share the costs of the legal intervention. With such limited prospects for cost-shifting, and with costs of the intervention in excess of the value of the intervention to the disadvantaged group, the disadvantaged group can be made worse off by the legal intervention

even though limits on wage and employment differentials are fully binding.

Christine Jolls, Antidiscrimination and Accommodation, 115 Harv. L. Rev. 642 (2001).

Should disparate impact law take account of differences in the make-up of labor pools? If a disadvantaged group constitutes a large enough fraction of a labor pool, such that there are too few nondisadvantaged employees on whom to spread the costs, should disparate impact still protect that pool? Would such a numerical cut-off for liability function like a quota defense? Finally, does this economic analysis suggest that employees who are entitled to accommodations for religious practices, pregnancy or physical disabilities might shoulder a disproportionately large fraction of the associated costs and thereby be made ''worse off'' by regulations that are intended to protect and support these employees?

Page 278.   Please insert the following case before part 3.

McClain v. Lufkin Indus., Inc.

519 F.3d 264 (5th Cir. 2008), cert. denied, ___ U.S. ___, 129 S.Ct. 198 (2008).

■ EDITH H. JONES, CHIEF JUDGE.

In this complex Title VII class action against Lufkin Industries, Inc., African–American plaintiffs allege that Lufkin's practice of delegating subjective decision-making authority to its managers with respect to initial assignments and promotions disparately affected them. After a bench trial, the district court issued a judgment in favor of the employees. After sifting through numerous issues, we reach results that are unfortunately inconclusive of the litigation. We affirm in part, reverse in part, and vacate and remand in part.

Lufkin, a large manufacturing corporation located in Lufkin, Texas, is divided into four production divisions: Foundry, Trailer, Oil Field, and Power Transmission. The company employs approximately 1,500 hourly and salaried workers, and the hourly workers have been unionized for many years.

Only two of the representative plaintiffs in this class action filed EEOC complaints. Sylvester McClain, the named plaintiff, began working in Lufkin's Trailer division in 1972. In January 1995, he complained to the EEOC that his supervisor, Arden Jinkins, had discriminated against him based on his race. Among other things, McClain complained that Jinkins tried to have him demoted. Buford Thomas, a Lufkin employee since 1979, filed his EEOC charge in February 1997, a year after he was allegedly constructively discharged. Thomas complained of being denied promotional and training opportunities because of his race while working in the Power

Transmission and Oil Field divisions. The EEOC issued right-to-sue letters on both charges.

McClain and Thomas sued Lufkin for employment discrimination in violation of Title VII and 42 U.S.C. § 1981. The plaintiffs asserted that systematic racial discrimination pervades Lufkin's initial job assignments, training, promotions, and compensation. The district court certified the plaintiffs' disparate-impact claims as a class action involving 700 current and former Lufkin employees. The class was described as:

> All Black persons employed for any period of time by defendant Lufkin Industries on or after March 6, 1994, to date, whose compensation, remuneration, benefits, job assignments, promotional opportunities, career advancements and other terms and conditions of employment have been, may have been, or may become, adversely affected by defendant Lufkin Industries' past or present systems of administering hiring, wages, salaries, job assignments, training, evaluations, promotions, demotions, terminations, layoffs, recalls, and rehires.

The court, however, declined to certify a disparate treatment class. Two claims went to trial: (1) discrimination against blacks in Lufkin's assignment of newly hired employees; and (2) racially discriminatory promotion practices that rested on largely subjective decision-making criteria carried out by a largely white supervisory corps.

Protracted pretrial proceedings in this case included two class certification hearings, two interlocutory appeals to this court, and a two-year mediation effort. When the case finally went to bench trial, the court strictly limited each party to twenty hours for the presentation of its case. Ultimately, the district court found that Lufkin's practice of delegating subjective decision-making authority to its white managers with respect to initial assignments and promotions resulted in a disparate impact on black employees in violation of Title VII. The court awarded the plaintiffs over $3.4 million in back pay, as well as attorneys' fees and injunctive relief. Both parties appeal.

* * *

Lufkin challenges two factual findings underlying the court's liability determination: that its decision-making process is subjective; and that its decision-making process could not be separated for analysis into components that were objective and non-racially biased. We address each in turn.

* * *

At Lufkin, promotions within the hourly ranks are putatively governed by a Collective Bargaining Agreement ("CBA") between Lufkin and three unions. Under the CBA, the company must post bid sheets for each new hourly opening. Seniority is the main criterion for promotion. However, plaintiffs offered evidence that promotions are not rigidly awarded according to seniority. Class members Sylvester McClain and Florine Thompson testified that they were personally bypassed for promotion in favor of a less senior white employee. Plaintiffs presented additional evidence that approximately half of all promotions were not awarded to the most senior bidder.

Moreover, the Collective Bargaining Agreement ("CBA") contains an ability clause that allowed Lufkin to fill positions on the basis of ability, regardless of seniority. The evidence indicates that ability determinations were not governed by objective standards. Paul Perez, Lufkin's Vice President of Human Resources, agreed that the ability determination was subjective. McClain testified that supervisors did not always truly evaluate ability when awarding promotions under the ability clause, but simply gave the position to the candidate they favored. Billy Webb, the union's chief spokesman, testified that the union had taken issue with the ability provision in past contract negotiations because it did not think that the ability clause was always administered fairly. The CBA also provides for a ten-day trial period following promotion. According to the testimony of one of its managers, Lufkin has no written guidelines or formal tests for determining which employees pass this trial period.

Plaintiffs also offered evidence that Lufkin permitted its managers to apportion training opportunities subjectively, a process that disadvantaged black employees who sought promotions. Perez testified that the CBA does not govern employees' daily work assignments, and he acknowledged that daily job assignments are not made on the basis of seniority. Perez testified that there are no written policies determining who is to receive on-the-job training, and Lufkin does not track how such training is allocated among employees. In addition, McClain testified that white employees were given more training in areas that were relevant to the jobs he sought. McClain explained that when "white managers and supervisors ... see a man they want to put on a particular job, ... they'll tap him" for training after his shift, or for external training. According to McClain, the employee who received the extra training would be the most qualified and would therefore receive the promotion once the job became available.

The district court also heard testimony that Lufkin's allegedly objective measures for determining which employees were eligible to bid, such as attendance and discipline records, are subject to variance and manipulation. Lufkin has a computer program that tracks attendance, but both McClain and Thompson testified that the system was manipulable. If an employee was absent or tardy and the supervisor did not want the employee to lose credit, Thompson stated that the supervisor could non-schedule the employee or use the employee's vacation days to skew the records. With respect to discipline records, Steve Reynolds, a Lufkin supervisor, testified that there are no written criteria for determining when a rule violation should be "written up." He stated that this decision is left to individual supervisors.

The evidence also supported that Lufkin engaged in subjective decision making when awarding promotions in the salaried ranks. Salaried positions are not governed by the CBA, and company managers admitted that they were unaware of any guidelines, criteria, or documentation for the process of making promotions to salaried positions. Rather, most promotions in the salaried ranks are awarded through an interview process.

In light of this evidence, we are not left with the definite and firm conviction that the district court erred in finding subjective decision making in Lufkin's promotion system.

* * *

Lufkin also challenges the district court's finding that its promotion practices are not capable of separation for review. Lufkin argues that if the court had isolated the objective factors in promotions—e.g. Lufkin's bidding practices and seniority—the court could not have found a discriminatory impact. As explained above, Title VII permits a plaintiff to demonstrate that the elements of the employer's decision-making process are not capable of separation for analysis and thus that the process should be analyzed as one employment practice. This court has not addressed the precise conditions under which employment practices are "not capable of separation for analysis." But "where a promotion system uses tightly integrated and overlapping criteria, it may be difficult as a practical matter for plaintiffs to isolate the particular step responsible for the observed discrimination."

* * *

There is no indication that the district court applied incorrect legal principles in determining that Lufkin's practices were incapable of separation. This finding of fact must be reviewed for clear error. Lufkin lists various ways in which its employment practices were analytically separable, but the court's express findings preclude separation according to those factors.

Lufkin argues, for example, that the plaintiffs' expert could have separated the challenged employment practices from its legitimate seniority system. The expert included in his analysis numerous promotions that contributed to the statistical shortfall in black promotions, even though these jobs were indisputably awarded to the most senior candidate. This argument ignores the district court's finding that Lufkin affords management considerable discretion in deciding whether to follow seniority in promotions. Plaintiffs could not statistically analyze the actual practice they challenge—subjective and discretionary application of the seniority provisions—by excluding promotion based on seniority. Seniority, the court found, was likely to have been irrelevant to the promotion.

Lufkin also contends that the plaintiffs should have separated out instances in which candidates were properly denied promotions because of unsatisfactory attendance. This argument, too, runs afoul of the court's finding that managers have substantial discretion in applying attendance rules. In such a system, a denial of promotion for poor attendance is not helpful to Lufkin where promotions may also have been awarded following non-uniform interpretation of employee attendance rules.

Finally, Lufkin contends that its "paper bid sheets provided additional information that plaintiffs could have separated for analysis." To the contrary, the district court rejected the bid data, which Lufkin prepared for purposes of this litigation, as unreliable and incomplete; ample evidence supports this finding.

Lufkin has not suggested any viable way, consistent with the court's findings, in which the plaintiffs could have separated the promotion criteria for review nor has it shown the district court clearly erred in so finding.

Lufkin maintains that the plaintiffs failed to demonstrate a statistically significant disparate impact against black employees in promotions. At trial, plaintiffs provided statistical evidence of discrimination through the report of their expert, Dr. Richard Drogin. After constructing hypothetical pools of employees who would be eligible for promotion, Dr. Drogin found that during the class period, black employees received 127 fewer hourly promotions and 8.85 fewer salaried promotions than should have been expected given their representation in these pools. Dr. Drogin determined that these differences were statistically significant at 7.61 standard deviations for hourly promotions and at 2.02 standard deviations for salaried promotions. In rebuttal, Lufkin offered the statistical analysis of Dr. Mary Baker. Dr. Baker conducted her calculations using bid data from Lufkin's paper bid sheets, and concluded that there was no statistically significant disparity in the promotion of blacks to hourly or salaried positions. Faced with this battle of experts, the district judge credited the testimony of Dr. Drogin over that of Dr. Baker.

* * *

Lufkin argues that even if the bid sheets were unavailable, Dr. Drogin's regression analysis would still be insufficient because his hypothetical applicant pools do not take into account other minimum qualifications of applicants, such as education. However, in selecting an appropriate pool and performing regression analysis in Title VII cases, the Supreme Court has taught that a plaintiff's regression analysis need not include "all measurable variables." A plaintiff in a Title VII suit need not prove discrimination with scientific certainty; rather his or her burden is to prove discrimination by a preponderance of the evidence. We are satisfied that Dr. Drogin's regression analysis was sufficiently refined for plaintiffs to meet this burden.

* * *

Lufkin also challenges the class-wide back-pay award. The district court's calculation of a back pay award is reviewed for clear error.

Lufkin complains that the district court erred by using a formula to calculate the award rather than computing damages on an individual basis. The complexity of the case is the determining factor in what method the district court should utilize to formulate a back-pay award. Whenever possible, back pay should be awarded individually and tailored to the actual victims of discrimination. If the class is small, the time period short, or the effect of the discrimination straightforward, individual determinations of each claimant's position but for the discrimination are possible. If, however, the class is large, the promotion or hiring practices are ambiguous, or the illegal practices continued over an extended period of time, a class-wide approach to the measure of back pay may be necessary.

In this case, the district court concluded that the size of the class and the inherent uncertainty of the individual claims contraindicates the use of an individualized approach. We agree. We are not persuaded that the district court could "easily" make individualized inquiries for each of the more than 700 plaintiffs in this case, as Lufkin contends. Further, there is no practical way to determine through individual hearings which jobs the class members would have bid on and obtained but for the discriminatory procedures Lufkin had in place. Class members outnumber promotion vacancies; jobs become available over time; the vacancies involve different pay rates; and a determination of who was entitled to a vacancy would have to be made by an evaluation of seniority and ability at that time. "[W]here employees start at entry level jobs in a department and progress into a myriad of other positions and departments on the basis of seniority and ability over an extended period of time, exact reconstruction of each individual claimant's work history, as if discrimination had not occurred, is not only imprecise but impractical." An individualized process of determining actual damages for each plaintiff in this case would result in the "quagmire of hypothetical judgments" that courts should avoid. Accordingly, the district court neither abused its discretion nor clearly erred in adopting the formula-driven approach.

The district court struggled to complete its work in this wide-ranging, complex discrimination case. Nevertheless, the sum of the foregoing discussion leaves much to be reconsidered. First, we vacate the judgment insofar as it holds Lufkin liable for a claim, unexhausted before the EEOC, that the company discriminatorily assigned newly hired African Americans to the Foundry division. Second, we affirm the judgment of Lufkin's liability to the class for the discriminatory impact of its subjective promotional policies. Because of this split decision, we must vacate and remand the damage award for further proceedings consistent with the foregoing discussion, as well as the award of injunctive relief and attorneys' fees.

AFFIRMED IN PART, REVERSED IN PART, VACATED AND REMANDED IN PART.

B. PROCEDURE

1. FILING A CHARGE OF EMPLOYMENT DISCRIMINATION

Page 301. Please insert the following.

5. In Halpert v. Manhattan Apartments, Inc., 580 F.3d 86 (2d Cir. 2009), the Second Circuit held that an employer may not escape liability for discriminatory acts by delegating those acts to an ostensibly independent agent. After Halpert applied for a position at Manhattan Apartments, he completed an interview with a "hiring agent" named Brooks. Halpert sued after Brooks allegedly told him during the interview that he was "too old" for the position. Ruling in favor of Halpert, the court found that Brooks was "acting as the hiring agent or apparent hiring agent [of Manhattan Apartments]" as opposed to "hiring on his own account."

Ledbetter v. Goodyear Tire & Rubber Co., Inc.

550 U.S. 618 (2007).

■ JUSTICE ALITO delivered the opinion of the Court.

This case calls upon us to apply established precedent in a slightly different context. We have previously held that the time for filing a charge of employment discrimination with the Equal Employment Opportunity Commission (EEOC) begins when the discriminatory act occurs. We have explained that this rule applies to any "[d]iscrete ac[t]" of discrimination, including discrimination in "termination, failure to promote, denial of transfer, [and] refusal to hire." Because a pay-setting decision is a "discrete act," it follows that the period for filing an EEOC charge begins when the act occurs. Petitioner, having abandoned her claim under the Equal Pay Act, asks us to deviate from our prior decisions in order to permit her to assert her claim under Title VII. Petitioner also contends that discrimination in pay is different from other types of employment discrimination and thus should be governed by a different rule. But because a pay-setting decision is a discrete act that occurs at a particular point in time, these arguments must be rejected. We therefore affirm the judgment of the Court of Appeals.

Petitioner Lilly Ledbetter worked for respondent Goodyear Tire and Rubber Company at its Gadsden, Alabama, plant from 1979 until 1998. During much of this time, salaried employees at the plant were given or denied raises based on their supervisors' evaluation of their performance. In March 1998, Ledbetter submitted a questionnaire to the EEOC alleging certain acts of sex discrimination, and in July of that year she filed a formal EEOC charge. After taking early retirement in November 1998, Ledbetter commenced this action, in which she asserted, among other claims, a Title

VII pay discrimination claim and a claim under the Equal Pay Act of 1963 (EPA).

The District Court granted summary judgment in favor of Goodyear on several of Ledbetter's claims, including her Equal Pay Act claim, but allowed others, including her Title VII pay discrimination claim, to proceed to trial. In support of this latter claim, Ledbetter introduced evidence that during the course of her employment several supervisors had given her poor evaluations because of her sex, that as a result of these evaluations her pay was not increased as much as it would have been if she had been evaluated fairly, and that these past pay decisions continued to affect the amount of her pay throughout her employment. Toward the end of her time with Goodyear, she was being paid significantly less than any of her male colleagues. Goodyear maintained that the evaluations had been non-discriminatory, but the jury found for Ledbetter and awarded her backpay and damages.

On appeal, Goodyear contended that Ledbetter's pay discrimination claim was time barred with respect to all pay decisions made prior to September 26, 1997—that is, 180 days before the filing of her EEOC questionnaire. And Goodyear argued that no discriminatory act relating to Ledbetter's pay occurred after that date.

The Court of Appeals for the Eleventh Circuit reversed, holding that a Title VII pay discrimination claim cannot be based on any pay decision that occurred prior to the last pay decision that affected the employee's pay during the EEOC charging period. The Court of Appeals then concluded that there was insufficient evidence to prove that Goodyear had acted with discriminatory intent in making the only two pay decisions that occurred within that time span, namely, a decision made in 1997 to deny Ledbetter a raise and a similar decision made in 1998.

* * *

In addressing the issue whether an EEOC charge was filed on time, we have stressed the need to identify with care the specific employment practice that is at issue. Ledbetter points to two different employment practices as possible candidates. Primarily, she urges us to focus on the paychecks that were issued to her during the EEOC charging period (the 180–day period preceding the filing of her EEOC questionnaire), each of which, she contends, was a separate act of discrimination. Alternatively, Ledbetter directs us to the 1998 decision denying her a raise, and she argues that this decision was "unlawful because it carried forward intentionally discriminatory disparities from prior years." Both of these arguments fail because they would require us in effect to jettison the defining element of the legal claim on which her Title VII recovery was based.

Ledbetter asserted disparate treatment, the central element of which is discriminatory intent. However, Ledbetter does not assert that the relevant Goodyear decisionmakers acted with actual discriminatory intent either when they issued her checks during the EEOC charging period or when they denied her a raise in 1998. Rather, she argues that the paychecks were unlawful because they would have been larger if she had been evaluated in a nondiscriminatory manner prior to the EEOC charging period. Similarly, she maintains that the 1998 decision was unlawful because it "carried forward" the effects of prior, uncharged discrimination decisions.

* * *

The instruction provided by [prior cases] is clear. The EEOC charging period is triggered when a discrete unlawful practice takes place. A new violation does not occur, and a new charging period does not commence, upon the occurrence of subsequent nondiscriminatory acts that entail adverse effects resulting from the past discrimination. But of course, if an employer engages in a series of acts each of which is intentionally discriminatory, then a fresh violation takes place when each act is committed.

* * *

Ledbetter's attempt to take the intent associated with the prior pay decisions and shift it to the 1998 pay decision is unsound. It would shift intent from one act (the act that consummates the discriminatory employment practice) to a later act that was not performed with bias or discriminatory motive. The effect of this shift would be to impose liability in the absence of the requisite intent.

* * *

The EEOC filing deadline "protect[s] employers from the burden of defending claims arising from employment decisions that are long past." Certainly, the 180–day EEOC charging deadline is short by any measure, but "[b]y choosing what are obviously quite short deadlines, Congress clearly intended to encourage the prompt processing of all charges of employment discrimination." This short deadline reflects Congress' strong preference for the prompt resolution of employment discrimination allegations through voluntary conciliation and cooperation.

A disparate-treatment claim comprises two elements: an employment practice, and discriminatory intent. Nothing in Title VII supports treating the intent element of Ledbetter's claim any differently from the employment practice element. If anything, concerns regarding stale claims weigh more heavily with respect to proof of the intent associated with employment practices than with the practices themselves. For example, in a case such as this in which the plaintiff's claim concerns the denial of raises, the employer's challenged acts (the decisions not to increase the employee's pay at the times in question) will almost always be documented and will typically not even be in dispute. By contrast, the employer's intent is almost always disputed, and evidence relating to intent may fade quickly with time. In most disparate-treatment cases, much if not all of the evidence of intent is circumstantial. Thus, the critical issue in a case involving a long-past performance evaluation will often be whether the evaluation was so far off the mark that a sufficient inference of discriminatory intent can be drawn. This can be a subtle determination, and the passage of time may seriously diminish the ability of the parties and the factfinder to reconstruct what actually happened.[4]

Ledbetter's policy arguments for giving special treatment to pay claims find no support in the statute and are inconsistent with our precedents. We apply the statute as written, and this means that any unlawful employment practice, including those involving compensation, must be presented to the EEOC within the period prescribed by statute.

For these reasons, the judgment of the Court of Appeals for the Eleventh Circuit is affirmed.

■ JUSTICE GINSBURG, with whom JUSTICE STEVENS, JUSTICE SOUTER, and JUSTICE BREYER join, dissenting.

Lilly Ledbetter was a supervisor at Goodyear Tire and Rubber's plant in Gadsden, Alabama, from 1979 until her retirement in 1998. For most of those years, she worked as an area manager, a position largely occupied by men. Initially, Ledbetter's salary was in line with the salaries of men performing substantially similar work. Over time, however, her pay slipped in comparison to the pay of male area managers with equal or less seniority. By the end of 1997, Ledbetter was the only woman working as an area manager and the pay discrepancy between Ledbetter and her 15 male counterparts was stark: Ledbetter was paid $3,727 per month; the lowest paid male area manager received $4,286 per month, the highest paid, $5,236.

* * *

The Court's insistence on immediate contest overlooks common characteristics of pay discrimination. Pay disparities often occur, as they did in Ledbetter's case, in small increments; cause to suspect that discrimination is at work develops only over time. Comparative pay information, moreover, is often hidden from the employee's view. Employers may keep under wraps the pay differentials maintained among supervisors, no less the reasons for those differentials. Small initial discrepancies may not be seen as meet for a federal case, particularly when the employee, trying to succeed in a nontraditional environment, is averse to making waves.

---

4. The dissent dismisses this concern, but this case illustrates the problems created by tardy lawsuits. Ledbetter's claims of sex discrimination turned principally on the misconduct of a single Goodyear supervisor, who, Ledbetter testified, retaliated against her when she rejected his sexual advances during the early 1980's, and did so again in the mid– 1990's when he falsified deficiency reports about her work. His misconduct, Ledbetter argues, was "a principal basis for [her] performance evaluation in 1997." Yet, by the time of trial, this supervisor had died and therefore could not testify. A timely charge might have permitted his evidence to be weighed contemporaneously.

Pay disparities are thus significantly different from adverse actions "such as termination, failure to promote, ... or refusal to hire," all involving fully communicated discrete acts, "easy to identify" as discriminatory. It is only when the disparity becomes apparent and sizable, e.g., through future raises calculated as a percentage of current salaries, that an employee in Ledbetter's situation is likely to comprehend her plight and, therefore, to complain. Her initial readiness to give her employer the benefit of the doubt should not preclude her from later challenging the then current and continuing payment of a wage depressed on account of her sex.

On questions of time under Title VII, we have identified as the critical inquiries: "What constitutes an 'unlawful employment practice' and when has that practice 'occurred'?" Our precedent suggests, and lower courts have overwhelmingly held, that the unlawful practice is the current payment of salaries infected by gender-based (or race-based) discrimination—a practice that occurs whenever a paycheck delivers less to a woman than to a similarly situated man.

* * *

Ledbetter's petition presents a question important to the sound application of Title VII: What activity qualifies as an unlawful employment practice in cases of discrimination with respect to compensation. One answer identifies the pay-setting decision, and that decision alone, as the unlawful practice. Under this view, each particular salary-setting decision is discrete from prior and subsequent decisions, and must be challenged within 180 days on pain of forfeiture. Another response counts both the pay-setting decision and the actual payment of a discriminatory wage as unlawful practices. Under this approach, each payment of a wage or salary infected by sex-based discrimination constitutes an unlawful employment practice; prior decisions, outside the 180–day charge-filing period, are not themselves actionable, but they are relevant in determining the lawfulness of conduct within the period. The Court adopts the first view, but the second is more faithful to precedent, more in tune with the realities of the workplace, and more respectful of Title VII's remedial purpose.

* * *

Pay disparities, of the kind Ledbetter experienced, have a closer kinship to hostile work environment claims than to charges of a single episode of discrimination. Ledbetter's claim rested not on one particular paycheck, but on "the cumulative effect of individual acts." She charged insidious discrimination building up slowly but steadily. Initially in line with the salaries of men performing substantially the same work, Ledbetter's salary fell 15 to 40 percent behind her male counterparts only after successive evaluations and percentage-based pay adjustments. Over time, she alleged and proved, the repetition of pay decisions undervaluing her work gave rise to the current discrimination of which she complained.

Though component acts fell outside the charge-filing period, with each new paycheck, Goodyear contributed incrementally to the accumulating harm.

The realities of the workplace reveal why the discrimination with respect to compensation that Ledbetter suffered does not fit within the category of singular discrete acts "easy to identify." A worker knows immediately if she is denied a promotion or transfer, if she is fired or refused employment. And promotions, transfers, hirings, and firings are generally public events, known to co-workers. When an employer makes a decision of such open and definitive character, an employee can immediately seek out an explanation and evaluate it for pretext. Compensation disparities, in contrast, are often hidden from sight. It is not unusual, decisions in point illustrate, for management to decline to publish employee pay levels, or for employees to keep private their own salaries. Tellingly, as the record in this case bears out, Goodyear kept salaries confidential; employees had only limited access to information regarding their colleagues' earnings.

The problem of concealed pay discrimination is particularly acute where the disparity arises not because the female employee is flatly denied a raise but because male counterparts are given larger raises. Having received a pay increase, the female employee is unlikely to discern at once that she has experienced an adverse employment decision. She may have little reason even to suspect discrimination until a pattern develops incrementally and she ultimately becomes aware of the disparity. Even if an employee suspects that the reason for a comparatively low raise is not performance but sex (or another protected ground), the amount involved may seem too small, or the employer's intent too ambiguous, to make the issue immediately actionable—or winnable.

Further separating pay claims from the discrete employment actions, an employer gains from sex-based pay disparities in a way it does not from a discriminatory denial of promotion, hiring, or transfer. When a male employee is selected over a female for a higher level position, someone still gets the promotion and is paid a higher salary; the employer is not enriched. But when a woman is paid less than a similarly situated man, the employer reduces its costs each time the pay differential is implemented. Furthermore, decisions on promotions, like decisions installing seniority systems, often implicate the interests of third-party employees in a way that pay differentials do not. Disparate pay, by contrast, can be remedied at any time solely at the expense of the employer who acts in a discriminatory fashion.

* * *

To show how far the Court has strayed from interpretation of Title VII with fidelity to the Act's core purpose, I return to the evidence Ledbetter presented at trial. Ledbetter proved to the jury the following: She was a member of a protected class; she performed work substantially equal to work of the dominant class (men); she was compensated less for that work; and the disparity was attributable to gender-based discrimination.

Specifically, Ledbetter's evidence demonstrated that her current pay was discriminatorily low due to a long series of decisions reflecting Goodyear's pervasive discrimination against women managers in general and Ledbetter in particular. Ledbetter's former supervisor, for example, admitted to the jury that Ledbetter's pay, during a particular one-year period, fell below Goodyear's minimum threshold for her position. Although Goodyear claimed the pay disparity was due to poor performance, the supervisor acknowledged that Ledbetter received a "Top Performance Award" in 1996. The jury also heard testimony that another supervisor—who evaluated Ledbetter in 1997 and whose evaluation led to her most recent raise denial—was openly biased against women. And two women who had previously worked as managers at the plant told the jury they had been subject to pervasive discrimination and were paid less than their male counterparts. One was paid less than the men she supervised. Ledbetter herself testified about the discriminatory animus conveyed to her by plant officials. Toward the end of her career, for instance, the plant manager told Ledbetter that the "plant did not need women, that [women] didn't help it, [and] caused problems."[10] After weighing all the evidence, the jury found for Ledbetter, concluding that the pay disparity was due to intentional discrimination.

Yet, under the Court's decision, the discrimination Ledbetter proved is not redressable under Title VII. Each and every pay decision she did not immediately challenge wiped the slate clean. Consideration may not be given to the cumulative effect of a series of decisions that, together, set her pay well below that of every male area manager. Knowingly carrying past pay discrimination forward must be treated as lawful conduct. Ledbetter may not be compensated for the lower pay she was in fact receiving when she complained to the EEOC. Nor, were she still employed by Goodyear, could she gain, on the proof she presented at trial, injunctive relief requiring, prospectively, her receipt of the same compensation men receive for substantially similar work. The Court's approbation of these consequences is totally at odds with the robust protection against workplace discrimination Congress intended Title VII to secure.

This is not the first time the Court has ordered a cramped interpretation of Title VII, incompatible with the statute's broad remedial purpose. See also Wards Cove Packing Co. v. Atonio (Casebook p. 267) (superseded in part by the Civil Rights Act of 1991); Price Waterhouse v. Hopkins (Casebook p. 232); 1 B. Lindemann & P. Grossman, Employment Discrimination Law 2 (3d ed. 1996) ("A spate of Court decisions in the late 1980s drew congressional fire and resulted in demands for legislative change[,]" culminating in the 1991 Civil Rights.) Once again, the ball is in Congress'

---

10. Given this abundant evidence, the Court cannot tenably maintain that Ledbet- ter's case "turned principally on the misconduct of a single Goodyear supervisor."

court. As in 1991, the Legislature may act to correct this Court's parsimonious reading of Title VII.

* * *

For the reasons stated, I would hold that Ledbetter's claim is not time barred and would reverse the Eleventh Circuit's judgment.

NOTES

1. The Lilly Ledbetter Fair Pay Act of 2009, one of the first statutes signed by President Obama, overturned the Supreme Court decision. It amended Title VII, the ADEA, and the ADA "to clarify that a discriminatory compensation decision . . . occurs each time compensation is paid pursuant to the discriminatory compensation decision." For Title VII actions, a successful plaintiff will be entitled to back pay for up to two years preceding the filing of the charge.

2. Compare *Ledbetter* with Lewis v. Chicago, 130 S.Ct. 1499 (2010), in which the Court considered the analogous issue of defining discriminatory acts in the context of employment tests. In *Lewis*, the Chicago Fire Department used a written test in its process for selecting new firefighters. Each administration of the test produced a list of candidates ranked by score, and each set of rankings remained valid for several rounds of hiring. In each round, the fire department filled vacant positions essentially by selecting the highest-ranking candidate remaining on the list. In addition to ranking candidates, the fire department defined a cutoff score, below which no candidate could qualify for employment. The plaintiff candidates argued that the cutoff score disproportionately eliminated minorities and that every round of hiring following an instance of the test gave rise to a fresh claim for disparate impact. Agreeing with the plaintiffs, the Court stated that "[i]t may be true that the City's * * * decision to adopt the cutoff score * * * gave rise to a freestanding disparate-impact claim. * * * But it does not follow that no new violation occurred * * * when the City implemented that decision down the road [in subsequent rounds of hiring]."

3. Professor Charles Sullivan argues that the Fair Pay Act ("FPA") has the potential to radically change the landscape for litigating claims under Title VII and other antidiscrimination laws. Charles A. Sullivan, Raising the Dead? The Lilly Ledbetter Fair Pay Act (June 11, 2009), Seton Hall Public Law Research Paper No. 1418101. Available at SSRN: http://ssrn.com/abstract=1418101. According to Sullivan, the radical implications of the Act, including its retroactive application and the removal of the statute of limitations for any practice affecting compensation, are the correct interpretation of the law. He rejected the constitutional challenges to FPA but recognized that the defense of laches may limit the impact of the new law.

4. When is an employee's EEOC intake form or affidavit considered a "charge" as required by the ADEA? The Supreme Court, in Federal Express Corp. v. Holowecki, 552 U.S. 389 (2008), adopted the EEOC's standard: to be deemed a "charge" under the ADEA, the filing must be reasonably construed as a request for the agency to take action to vindicate the employee's rights. Justice Thomas, former head of the EEOC, filed a dissenting opinion, joined by Justice Scalia. The dissent argued that the Court's decision "absolves the EEOC of its obligation to administer the ADEA according to discernible standards," and that an intake form should not be considered a charge unless it "objectively indicates an intent to initiate the EEOC's enforcement process."

3.   PROVING DISCRIMINATION

Staub v. Proctor Hospital

560 F.3d 647 (7th Cir. 2009), cert. granted, ___ U.S. ___, 130 S.Ct. 2089 (2010).

■ EVANS, CIRCUIT JUDGE:

One would guess that the chances are pretty slim that the work of a 17th century French poet would find its way into a Chicago courtroom in 2009. But that's the situation in this case as we try to make sense out of what has been dubbed the "cat's paw" theory. The term derives from the fable "The Monkey and the Cat" penned by Jean de La Fontaine (1621–1695). In the tale, a clever—and rather unscrupulous—monkey persuades an unsuspecting feline to snatch chestnuts from a fire. The cat burns her paw in the process while the monkey profits, gulping down the chestnuts one by one. As understood today, a cat's paw is a "tool" or "one used by another to accomplish his purposes." Webster's Third New International Dictionary (1976). More on this a little later.

Vincent Staub sued the Proctor Hospital of Peoria, Illinois, under the Uniformed Services Employment and Reemployment Rights Act (US-ERRA), after he was discharged from his position as an angiography technologist. An Army reservist, Staub alleged that the reasons given—insubordination, shirking, and attitude problems—were just a pretext for discrimination based on his association with the military. A jury sided with Staub, and the district court denied Proctor's renewed motion for judgment as a matter of law or for a new trial. * * * [T]he cat's paw theory, which we will discuss later in more detail, is a way of proving discrimination when the decisionmaker herself is admittedly unbiased; under the theory, the discriminatory animus of a nondecisionmaker is imputed to the decisionmaker where the former has singular influence over the latter and uses that influence to cause the adverse employment action.

* * *

Staub was a veteran member of the United States Army Reserve. Like all reservists, he was a part-time soldier, spending the bulk of his hours in the civilian world. For Staub, that meant employment as an angio tech for Proctor. Balancing work and military duties can be a complicated task, but Staub apparently managed. For a while, at least. In late 2000, some 10 years after he was hired, things began to grow a little tense.

It was around that time that Janice Mulally, second in command of the Diagnostic Imaging Department, began to prepare the department work schedules. Staub would notify Mulally of his drill and training obligations, which occupied one weekend per month and two weeks during the summer. Before Mulally took over scheduling, Staub had weekends off. But Mulally placed Staub back in the weekend rotation, creating conflicts with his drill schedule.

* * *   Mulally made her reasons plain: She called Staub's military duties "bullshit" and said the extra shifts were his "way of paying back the department for everyone else having to bend over backwards to cover [his] schedule for the Reserves." And it came as no surprise that Korenchuk, [a high-ranking HR official], did little to remedy the situation. Although Korenchuk only commented about Staub's reserve duties on a "couple different occasions," these comments were none too subtle. Korenchuk characterized drill weekends as "Army Reserve bullshit" and "a bunch of smoking and joking and a waste of taxpayers' money."

Bad as that was, things became worse in 2003. In February of that year, Staub was called to active duty for a period of up to one year. Though unforeseen circumstances cut the tour short at the 92–day mark, Staub's return home was less than pleasant. Korenchuk told one of Staub's coworkers, Amy Knoerle, that Mulally was "out to get" Staub. Knoerle was at a loss because she saw nothing in Staub but a hard worker and team player. However, she noticed that whenever Staub approached Mulally about drill obligations, Mulally would roll her eyes and make sighing noises

* * *

[T]he tide was turning against Staub, and his military obligations were at least peripherally involved. On January 9, 2004, Staub received an order to report for "soldier readiness processing," a precursor to another round of active deployment. Staub gave a copy of the order to both Korenchuk and Mulally, and Korenchuk became apprehensive. He asked Staub several times per week when he would have to ship out. Day had resigned by this point, leaving Sweborg and Staub as the only two angio techs. If Staub went on active duty, Korenchuk would have to use "rent-a-techs," placing strain on the department's budget.

One might think this enhanced Staub's job security, but not so. On January 27, 2004, Mulally gave Staub a written warning accusing him of shirking his duties. A bit of background information is necessary to understand what Staub allegedly failed to do, because it bore no connection to angiography. The Diagnostic Imaging Department (headed by Koren-chuk) was divided into two units: one unit for angiography, and a far larger unit for traditional diagnostic imaging services like radiology, mammography, ultra sounds, CAT scans, and MRIs. Though they normally stuck to their speciality, angio techs were trained to work in both units and therefore had the ability to help out with radiology and the like when the need arose and the circumstances permitted. According to Mulally, however, Staub didn't respect that arrangement.

On the morning of January 26, a worker from general diagnostics called Mulally to see if any of the angio techs were free to help out. Mulally in turn called Sweborg and asked if she and Staub had any patients. Sweborg said they didn't and, according to Mulally, later admitted they were completely free from 8:30 to 9:45 a.m. Nevertheless, Sweborg and Staub failed to lend a hand. Mulally therefore issued Staub a written warning—Sweborg received one the next day—noting that he had already been warned about this behavior several times. But Staub and Sweborg dispute all that. They say they had an angio patient at 8:30 a.m., and although that case was ultimately cancelled by the doctor, they learned of the cancellation only 15 minutes prior to the call for help in general diagnostics, to which they immediately responded. Further, according to Sweborg and Staub, they had never before been instructed to report automatically to general diagnostics if they did not have angio cases. Staub thus refused to sign the warning, and he asked Korenchuk (who approved the action) why he was being targeted. Korenchuk said Mulally "had all of the pertinent facts," and he just signed the warning "to get her off of his back." So the warning stood, and so did its instructions for the future. Going forward, Staub was to "report to Mike [Korenchuk] or Jan [Mulally] when [he] ha[d] no patients and [the angio] cases [we]re complete[d]." He would also "remain in the general diagnostic area unless [he] specified to Mike or Jan where and why [he would] go elsewhere."

This discipline of Staub emboldened Mulally. Shortly afterwards she called Staub's Reserve Unit Administrator, Joseph Abbidini, in Bartonville, Illinois. Mulally had called Abbidini on a prior occasion to confirm that Staub was actually a member of the Reserves, but now she wanted to know if Staub could be excused from some of his military duties. Mulally asked Abbidini if Staub really had to attend two-week training in the summer because he was needed at work. Abbidini stated that the training was mandatory. Most Reserve members have outside employment, he explained, so excusing Staub would set an ugly precedent. Mulally's response? She called Abbadini an "asshole" and hung up.

* * *

The day of reckoning started out normally enough. Staub and Sweborg worked together in the angio department all morning, finishing up around lunchtime. Hungry, yet mindful of the prior warning, Staub walked to Korenchuk's office to tell him that he and Sweborg were going to lunch.

But Korenchuk wasn't there. So Staub walked back to the angio suite, placed a call to Korenchuk's office, and left a voice mail informing him they were off to the cafeteria. Staub and Sweborg returned 30 minutes later and went to work on some leftover filming. Korenchuk showed up a few moments afterwards, demanding to know where they had been. He said he was "looking all over" for Staub, and Staub's explanation—that they were only at lunch and left a voice mail—appeased him little. Korenchuk escorted Staub down to Buck's office in Human Resources, picking up a security guard along the way. Korenchuk had met with Buck, [head of HR], earlier in the day—informing her that Staub failed to report in as instructed and couldn't be located—so the decision to terminate was already made. As Staub walked into the room, Buck handed him his pink slip. The guard then escorted him off the grounds. Sweborg was not disciplined, though she resigned a few days later out of disgust.

According to the written notice, Staub was discharged for failing to heed the earlier warning instructing him to report to Korenchuk whenever he had no more work in the angio department and otherwise to remain in the general diagnostics area. Without the January 27 write-up, Day's April 2 complaint, and the event on April 20—all of which involved unavailability or "disappearances"—Buck said she would not have fired Staub. Buck's testimony makes it clear that although she relied on Korenchuk's input, the ultimate decision was hers. Korenchuk "reluctantly agreed" with her decision, but it was her call to make.

Beyond consulting Korenchuk and reviewing the more recent incidents, Buck relied on past issues with Staub in making her decision. She said she heard "frequent complaints" about Staub during her first year with Proctor, 2001. And she knew of two workers who resigned because of Staub in 2002: an angio tech quit because Staub made her feel like "gum on the bottom of his shoe," and a registered nurse gave up for similar reasons. What's more, a recruiter told Buck she had difficulty attracting workers to angio because Staub "had a reputation." Among other things, he was known for flirting with medical students.

Admittedly, however, Buck failed to speak with other angio techs who worked with Staub, including Sweborg, and she had no idea that Mulally and Day wanted Staub fired. But Buck did review Staub's employee file, including the good (like his most recent annual evaluation) and the bad (like the January 27 write-up)

* * *

Against this backdrop, Staub faced an uphill battle in his USERRA discrimination suit. Like other employment discrimination legislation, USERRA prohibits adverse action based on a prohibited criterion, in this case military status. But also as with other discrimination legislation, a plaintiff suing under USERRA does not win by showing prohibited animus by just anyone. He must show that the decisionmaker harbored animus and relied on that animus in choosing to take action. Since Buck was the decisionmaker and there was no evidence she had a problem with Staub on account of his membership in the Reserves, Staub was out of luck under the traditional rubric. But that doesn't mean he had no case at all.

Deploying the cat's paw theory, Staub sought to attribute Mulally's animus to Buck, and therefore to Proctor. He posited that Mulally fed false information to Buck (i.e., that he dodged work on January 26, 2004); that Mulally was motivated to do this because he was a member of the Army Reserves; and that Buck relied on this false information (without vetting it any meaningful way) in deciding to fire him. The case made it to trial on this theory, where the jury apparently found it convincing, returning a verdict in Staub's favor. Pursuant to the parties' stipulation, Staub was awarded $57,640 in damages. The court then denied Proctor's renewed motion for a new trial or judgment as a matter of law.

* * *

In Brewer [v. Board of Trustees of University, of Illinois, 479 F.3d 908 (7th Cir. 2007)], we applied the cat's paw concept to discrimination law. That case dealt with the "Machiavellian world of permit parking at the University of Illinois's Urbana-Champaign campus, and the ill fortune of a student who became involved in it." The student, Lonnell Brewer, was fired from his part-time job after he was caught with a modified parking tag. Brewer said his supervisor (Kerrin Thompson) gave him permission to modify the tag, and she kept this fact a secret because he was black and she wanted him fired. * * * Thompson, however, did not make the decision to terminate. The decision instead came from someone higher up the chain of command—Denise Hendricks—and there was no evidence that she harbored any racial animus * * * It wasn't fair to impute Thompson's animus to Hendricks, we concluded, because Hendricks looked into the situation for herself; though she "listened to the information Thompson relayed to her," she "did not simply rely on it." From this we derived a simple rule to prevent the cat's paw theory from spiraling out of control: "[W]here a decision maker is not wholly dependent on a single source of information, but instead conducts its own investigation into the facts relevant to the decision, the employer is not liable for an employee's submission of misinformation to the decision maker."

By asking whether the decisionmaker conducted her own investigation and analysis, we respected the role of the decisionmaker. We were, and remain to this day, unprepared to find an employer liable based on a nondecisionmaker's animus unless the "decisionmaker" herself held that title only nominally. If the decisionmaker wasn't used as a cat's paw—if she didn't just take the monkey's word for it, as it were—then of course the theory is not in play.

* * *

Staub's abundant evidence of Mulally's animosity was erroneously admitted into evidence. And this error was prejudicial because the strongest proof of anti-military sentiment came from the improperly admitted evidence.

* * *

The story told by the evidence is really quite plain. Apart from the friction caused by his military service, the evidence suggests that Staub, although technically competent, was prone to attitude problems. The fact that he made some friends along the way (such as Sweborg) doesn't diminish the fact that he offended numerous others for reasons unrelated to his participation in the Reserves. So, when Staub ran into trouble in the winter and spring of 2004, he didn't have the safety net of a good reputation. Even if Staub behaved reasonably on the day of his discharge and the January 27 write-up was exaggerated by Mulally, his track record nonetheless supported Buck's action. Most importantly, Buck took this action free of any military-based animus, which Staub admits. And the cat's paw is not applicable—even setting aside the evidentiary error—because a reasonable jury could not find that Mulally (or anyone else) had singular influence over Buck. To the contrary, the evidence established that Buck looked beyond what Mulally and Korenchuk said—remember, Korenchuk supported the firing only "reluctantly"—and determined that Staub was a liability to the company. We admit that Buck's investigation could have been more robust, e.g., she failed to pursue Staub's theory that Mulally fabricated the write-up; had Buck done this, she may have discovered that Mulally indeed bore a great deal of anti-military animus. But the rule we developed in Brewer does not require the decisionmaker to be a paragon of independence. It is enough that the decisionmaker "is not wholly dependent on a single source of information" and conducts her "own investigation into the facts relevant to the decision" To require much more than that would be to ignore the realities of the workplace. Decisionmakers usually have to rely on others' opinions to some extent because they are removed from the underlying situation. But to be a cat's paw requires more; true to the fable, it requires a blind reliance, the stuff of "singular influence." Buck was not a cat's paw for Mulally or anyone else. Although Mulally may have enjoyed seeing Staub fired due to his association with the military, this was not the reason he was fired. Viewing the evidence reasonably, it simply cannot be said that Buck did anything other than exercise her independent judgment, following a reasonable review of the facts, and simply decide that Staub was not a team player. We do not mean to suggest by all this that we agree with Buck's decision—it seems a bit harsh given Staub's upsides and tenure—but that is not the issue. The question for us is whether a reasonable jury could have concluded that Staub was fired because he was a member of the military. To that question, the answer is no.

NOTE

The claim in *Staub* was for discrimination on the basis of association with the military. The court described a cat's-paw claim as an argument that the ultimate decision-maker exhibited "blind reliance" on a subordinate employee whose motives were unlawfully discriminatory. To what extent does this standard of proof allow an employer to escape liability when the supervisor conducts a perfunctory "independent" investigation?

C. RETALIATION

Page 313. Please insert the following case.

Crawford v. Metropolitan Government of Nashville

___ U.S. ___, 129 S.Ct. 846 (2009).

■ JUSTICE SOUTER delivered the opinion of the Court.

Title VII of the Civil Rights Act of 1964 forbids retaliation by employers against employees who report workplace race or gender discrimination. The question here is whether this protection extends to an employee who speaks out about discrimination not on her own initiative, but in answering questions during an employer's internal investigation. We hold that it does.

In 2002, respondent Metropolitan Government of Nashville and Davidson County, Tennessee (Metro), began looking into rumors of sexual harassment by the Metro School District's employee relations director, Gene Hughes. When Veronica Frazier, a Metro human resources officer, asked petitioner Vicky Crawford, a 30–year Metro employee, whether she had witnessed "inappropriate behavior" on the part of Hughes, Crawford described several instances of sexually harassing behavior: once, Hughes had answered her greeting, " 'Hey Dr. Hughes, what's up?,' " by grabbing his crotch and saying " '[Y]ou know what's up' "; he had repeatedly " 'put his crotch up to[her] window' "; and on one occasion he had entered her office and " 'grabbed her head and pulled it to his crotch.' " Two other employees also reported being sexually harassed by Hughes. Although Metro took no action against Hughes, it did fire Crawford and the two other accusers soon after finishing the investigation, saying in Crawford's case that it was for embezzlement. Crawford claimed Metro was retaliating for her report of Hughes's behavior and filed a charge of a Title VII violation with the Equal Employment Opportunity Commission (EEOC), followed by this suit in the United States District Court for the Middle District of Tennessee.

The Title VII antiretaliation provision has two clauses, making it "an unlawful employment practice for an employer to discriminate against any of his employees ... [1] because he has opposed any practice made an unlawful employment practice by this subchapter, or [2] because he has made a charge, testified, assisted, or participated in any manner in an investigation, proceeding, or hearing under this subchapter." The one is known as the "opposition clause," the other as the "participation clause," and Crawford accused Metro of violating both.

The District Court granted summary judgment for Metro. It held that Crawford could not satisfy the opposition clause because she had not "instigated or initiated any complaint," but had "merely answered questions by investigators in an already-pending internal investigation, initiated by someone else." It concluded that her claim also failed under the participation clause, which Sixth Circuit precedent confined to protecting " 'an employee's participation in an employer's internal investigation . . . where that investigation occurs pursuant to a pending EEOC charge' " (not the case here).

The Court of Appeals affirmed on the same grounds, holding that the opposition clause " 'demands active, consistent "opposing" activities to warrant . . . protection against retaliation,' " whereas Crawford did "not claim to have instigated or initiated any complaint prior to her participation in the investigation, nor did she take any further action following the investigation and prior to her firing." Again like the trial judge, the Court of Appeals understood that Crawford could show no violation of the participation clause because her " 'employer's internal investigation' " was not conducted " 'pursuant to a pending EEOC charge.' "

* * *

The opposition clause makes it "unlawful . . . for an employer to discriminate against any . . . employe[e] . . . because he has opposed any practice made . . . unlawful . . . by this subchapter." The term "oppose" being left undefined by the statute, carries its ordinary meaning, "to resist or antagonize . . .; to contend against; to confront; resist; withstand," Webster's New International Dictionary 1710 (2d ed. 1958). Although these actions entail varying expenditures of energy, "RESIST frequently implies more active striving than OPPOSE." see also Random House Dictionary of the English Language 1359 (2d ed. 1987) (defining "oppose" as "to be hostile or adverse to, as in opinion").

The statement Crawford says she gave to Frazier is thus covered by the opposition clause, as an ostensibly disapproving account of sexually obnoxious behavior toward her by a fellow employee, an answer she says antagonized her employer to the point of sacking her on a false pretense. Crawford's description of the louche goings-on would certainly qualify in the minds of reasonable jurors as "resist[ant]" or "antagoni[stic]" to Hughes's treatment, if for no other reason than the point argued by the Government and explained by an EEOC guideline: "When an employee communicates to her employer a belief that the employer has engaged in . . . a form of employment discrimination, that communication" virtually always "constitutes the employee's opposition to the activity." It is true that one can imagine exceptions, like an employee's description of a supervisor's racist joke as hilarious, but these will be eccentric cases, and this is not one of them.

* * *

"Oppose" goes beyond "active, consistent" behavior in ordinary discourse, where we would naturally use the word to speak of someone who has taken no action at all to advance a position beyond disclosing it. Countless people were known to "oppose" slavery before Emancipation, or are said to "oppose" capital punishment today, without writing public letters, taking to the streets, or resisting the government. And we would call it "opposition" if an employee took a stand against an employer's discriminatory practices not by "instigating" action, but by standing pat, say, by refusing to follow a supervisor's order to fire a junior worker for discriminatory reasons. There is, then, no reason to doubt that a person can "oppose" by responding to someone else's question just as surely as by provoking the discussion, and nothing in the statute requires a freakish rule protecting an employee who reports discrimination on her own initiative but not one who reports the same discrimination in the same words when her boss asks a question.

* * *

If it were clear law that an employee who reported discrimination in answering an employer's questions could be penalized with no remedy, prudent employees would have a good reason to keep quiet about Title VII offenses against themselves or against others. This is no imaginary horrible given the documented indications that "[f]ear of retaliation is the leading reason why people stay silent instead of voicing their concerns about bias and discrimination." The appeals court's rule would thus create a real dilemma for any knowledgeable employee in a hostile work environment if the boss took steps to assure a defense under our cases. If the employee reported discrimination in response to the enquiries, the employer might well be free to penalize her for speaking up. But if she kept quiet about the discrimination and later filed a Title VII claim, the employer might well escape liability, arguing that it "exercised reasonable care to prevent and correct [any discrimination] promptly" but "the plaintiff employee unreasonably failed to take advantage of . . . preventive or corrective opportunities provided by the employer." Nothing in the statute's text or our precedent supports this catch–22.

* * *

The judgment of the Court of Appeals for the Sixth Circuit is reversed, and the case is remanded for further proceedings consistent with this opinion.

■ JUSTICE ALITO, with whom JUSTICE THOMAS joins, concurring in the judgment.

The question in this case is whether Title VII of the Civil Rights Act of 1964 prohibits retaliation against an employee who testifies in an internal investigation of alleged sexual harassment. I agree with the Court that the "opposition clause" prohibits retaliation for such conduct. I also agree with the Court's primary reasoning, which is based on the point argued by the Government and explained by an EEOC guideline: "When an employee communicates to her employer a belief that the employer has engaged in ... a form of employment discrimination, that communication virtually always 'constitutes the employee's opposition to the activity.' " I write separately to emphasize my understanding that the Court's holding does not and should not extend beyond employees who testify in internal investigations or engage in analogous purposive conduct.

Petitioner contends that the statutory term "oppose" means "taking action (including making a statement) to end, prevent, redress, or correct unlawful discrimination."

In order to decide the question that is before us, we have no need to adopt a definition of the term "oppose" that is broader than the definition that petitioner advances. But in dicta, the Court notes that the fourth listed definition in the Random House Dictionary of the English Language goes further, defining "oppose" to mean " 'to be hostile or adverse to, as in opinion.' " Thus, this definition embraces silent opposition.

While this is certainly an accepted usage of the term "oppose," the term is not always used in this sense, and it is questionable whether silent opposition is covered by the opposition clause of 42 U. S. C. § 2000e–3(a). It is noteworthy that all of the other conduct protected by this provision—making a charge, testifying, or assisting or participating in an investigation, proceeding, or hearing—requires active and purposive conduct.

An interpretation of the opposition clause that protects conduct that is not active and purposive would have important practical implications. It would open the door to retaliation claims by employees who never expressed a word of opposition to their employers. To be sure, in many cases, such employees would not be able to show that management was aware of their opposition and thus would not be able to show that their opposition caused the adverse actions at issue. But in other cases, such employees might well be able to create a genuine factual issue on the question of causation. Suppose, for example, that an employee alleges that he or she expressed opposition while informally chatting with a co-worker at the proverbial water cooler or in a workplace telephone conversation that was overheard by a co-worker. Or suppose that an employee alleges that such a conversation occurred after work at a restaurant or tavern frequented by co-workers or at a neighborhood picnic attended by a friend or relative of a supervisor. Some courts hold that an employee asserting a retaliation claim can prove causation simply by showing that the adverse employment action occurred within a short time after the protected conduct.

The number of retaliation claims filed with the EEOC has proliferated in recent years. An expansive interpretation of protected opposition conduct would likely cause this trend to accelerate.

The question whether the opposition clause shields employees who do not communicate their views to their employers through purposive conduct is not before us in this case; the answer to that question is far from clear; and I do not understand the Court's holding to reach that issue here. For present purposes, it is enough to hold that the opposition clause does protect an employee, like petitioner, who testifies about unlawful conduct in an internal investigation.

Page 318. Please add the following note.

2A. Can litigious conduct, such as lawsuits, counter-claims, or EEOC activity, be considered retaliatory conduct under the *Burlington* standard? Plaintiff filed a sexual harassment lawsuit against her employer and lost in court. When the employer responded by filing a tort claim alleging, among other things, abuse of process, malicious prosecution, and intentional infliction of emotional distress, the employee countered by filing a claim of retaliation. The Ohio Supreme Court held that the employer's counterclaim was not per se retaliatory, because it was not objectively baseless, and employers have a First Amendment right to seek relief in court. See Greer–Burger v. Temesi, 879 N.E.2d 174 (Ohio 2007).

Page 318. Please delete note 3 and insert the following notes.

3. Can an employer be liable for retaliation against an employee based on the protected activities of a third party? A 16–year–old girl working at a Burger King restaurant was being sexually harassed by her 35–year–old manager. After the employee's mother visited the restaurant to complain of her daughter's harassment, the harassing supervisor fired the employee. The Seventh Circuit referred to this as "third party retaliation": someone other than the victim complains about the harassment, and the employer responds by retaliating against the victim. If the third party is a "bystand-er" or "stranger" to the harassment, then the victim has no remedy for retaliation. However, if the third party is an agent of the victim, such as an attorney or, as in this case, a minor's parent or guardian, then the complaining party's actions may be attributed to the victim, and therefore the retaliation against the victim is actionable. See EEOC v. V & J Foods, 507 F.3d 575 (7th Cir. 2007). See also Baird ex rel. Baird v. Rose, 192 F.3d 462 (4th Cir. 1999) (permitting a claim on behalf of the child for retaliation based on parent-guardian conduct). The court in V & J Foods declined to decide whether an "intermediate" type of third-party retaliation, involving an informal representative or ad hoc agent of the victim, would be actionable.

3A. Can an employee claim retaliation if he or she is neither the victim nor the opposer of the original alleged act of discrimination? See Donato v. AT & T, 728 So.2d 201 (Fla. 1998), which held that the law does not protect a husband allegedly discharged because his wife sued their employer for sex discrimination. See also Thompson v. North Am. Stainless, LP, 567 F.3d 804 (6th Cir. 2009) (en banc), cert. granted, 130 S.Ct. ___ (2010). An employee was terminated after his coworker fiancee filed a gender discrimination charge with the EEOC. A three-judge panel of the Sixth Circuit said that the terminated employee could sue for unlawful retaliation. En banc, the court reversed by a vote of 10 to 6, the majority saying that the clear language of Title VII gave a retaliation cause of action only to an employee dismissed or otherwise disciplined because that employee engaged in protected activity.

3B.   Can a final decision-maker's wholly independent, legitimate decision to terminate an employee insulate from liability a lower-level supervisor involved in the process who had a retaliatory motive to have the employee fired? "[T]he answer must be yes, because the termination decision was not shown to be influenced by the subordinate's retaliatory motives." This was a section 1983 case, but the court said that the same result would be reached in a Title VII or an ADEA case. Lakeside–Scott v. Multnomah County, 556 F.3d 797 (9th Cir. 2009).

Page 319.   Please add the following notes.

5.   Courts must decide whether specific discrimination statutes create a cause of action for retaliation when the statutory text is silent on the question. In 2008, the Supreme Court interpreted two important statutes as granting such a right. The Court held that 42 U.S.C. § 1981, which grants "[a]ll persons . . . the same right . . . to make and enforce contracts . . . as is enjoyed by white citizens," encompasses retaliation claims. Justice Breyer's opinion for the majority relied heavily on stare decisis. Justice Thomas, in a dissent joined by Justice Scalia, argued that section 1981 only bars racial discrimination and that, for example, an employer who retaliates against both an African American and a white employee who each complain of racial discrimination would not be discriminating on the basis of race. CBOCS West, Inc. v. Humphrie, 553 U.S. 542 (2008). On the same day the Court held that the Age Discrimination in Employment Act also covers retaliation by the federal government. Gomez–Perez v. Potter, 553 U.S. 474 (2008), discussed infra.

6.   Retaliation plays a large part in many workplace harassment claims. Both causes of action can be supported by overlapping evidence, which causes problems for plaintiffs, courts, and scholars. For instance, if a female employee is denied a raise, brings suit against her employer, and then is subjected to severe and pervasive harsh treatment based on her sex, the later discrimination is at once retaliation and harassment. Some scholars suggest changing the doctrine to allow plaintiffs to bring hybrid harassment/retaliation claims, so that they can seek more complete relief. See, e.g., Eisha Jain, Note, Realizing the Potential of the Joint Harassment/Retaliation Claim, 117 Yale L.J. 120 (2007). For more on harassment, see Chapter 7, pp. 594–616.

7. An employer had a policy of denying or stopping its internal review of discrimination complaints once it learned that the complaining employee filed a charge with the EEOC or state agency. The Florida Supreme Court found that the employer's policy satisfies the "materially adverse" standard under *Burlington* because it dissuades reasonable employees from filing charges. See Donovan v. Broward County, 974 So.2d 458 (Fla. Ct. App. 2008).

8. In some retaliation cases, temporal proximity between the employee's protected activity and the employer's adverse employment action may suffice to establish causation. See Mickey v. Zeidler Tool & Die Co., 516 F.3d 516, 523–525 (6th Cir. 2008) ("[I]f an employer immediately retaliates against an employee upon learning of his protected activity, the employee would be unable to couple temporal proximity with any such other evidence of retaliation because the two actions happened consecutively.... Thus, employers who retaliate swiftly and immediately upon learning of protected activity would ironically have a stronger defense than those who delay in taking adverse retaliatory action.")

9. Retaliation is one of the most common employment discrimination charges filed, second only to race discrimination, according to EEOC statistics. About one-third of all EEOC charges filed include retaliation claims—an increase from 22.6% in 1997 to 32.3% in 2007. The total number of employment discrimination charges has risen from 75,000 in 2006 to 82,000 in 2007, the highest level since 2002. Why might these numbers be rising? See Charge Statistics From The U.S. Equal Employment Opportunity Commission FY 1997, available at http://www.eeoc.gov/stats/charges.html.

D. AFFIRMATIVE ACTION AND REVERSE DISCRIMINATION

Page 319. **Please replace *Lomack* with the following:**

Ricci v. DeStefano

129 S.Ct. 2658 (2009).

■ JUSTICE KENNEDY delivered the opinion of the Court.

When the City of New Haven undertook to fill vacant lieutenant and captain positions in its fire department (Department), the promotion and hiring process was governed by the city charter, in addition to federal and state law. The charter establishes a merit system. That system requires the City to fill vacancies in the classified civil-service ranks with the most qualified individuals, as determined by job-related examinations. After each examination, the New Haven Civil Service Board (CSB) certifies a ranked list of applicants who passed the test. Under the charter's "rule of three," the relevant hiring authority must fill each vacancy by choosing one candidate from the top three scorers on the list. Certified promotional lists remain valid for two years.

The City's contract with the New Haven firefighters' union specifies additional requirements for the promotion process. Under the contract, applicants for lieutenant and captain positions were to be screened using written and oral examinations, with the written exam accounting for 60 percent and the oral exam 40 percent of an applicant's total score. To sit for the examinations, candidates for lieutenant needed 30 months' experience in the Department, a high-school diploma, and certain vocational training courses. Candidates for captain needed one year's service as a lieutenant in the Department, a high-school diploma, and certain vocational training courses.

After reviewing bids from various consultants, the City hired Industrial/Organizational Solutions, Inc. (IOS) to develop and administer the examinations, at a cost to the City of $100,000. IOS is an Illinois company that specializes in designing entry-level and promotional examinations for fire and police departments.

* * *

Candidates took the examinations in November and December 2003. Seventy-seven candidates completed the lieutenant examination—43 whites, 19 blacks, and 15 Hispanics. Of those, 34 candidates passed—25 whites, 6 blacks, and 3 Hispanics. Eight lieutenant positions were vacant at the time of the examination. As the rule of three operated, this meant that the top 10 candidates were eligible for an immediate promotion to lieutenant. All 10 were white. Subsequent vacancies would have allowed at least 3 black candidates to be considered for promotion to lieutenant.

Forty-one candidates completed the captain examination—25 whites, 8 blacks, and 8 Hispanics. Of those, 22 candidates passed—16 whites, 3 blacks, and 3 Hispanics. Seven captain positions were vacant at the time of the examination. Under the rule of three, 9 candidates were eligible for an immediate promotion to captain—7 whites and 2 Hispanics.

The City's contract with IOS contemplated that, after the examinations, IOS would prepare a technical report that described the examination processes and methodologies and analyzed the results. But in January 2004, rather than requesting the technical report, City officials, including the City's counsel, Thomas Ude, convened a meeting with IOS Vice President Chad Legel. (Legel was the leader of the IOS team that developed and administered the tests.) Based on the test results, the City officials expressed concern that the tests had discriminated against minority candidates. Legel defended the examinations' validity, stating that any numerical disparity between white and minority candidates was likely due to various external factors and was in line with results of the Department's previous promotional examinations.

* * *

At the close of witness testimony, the CSB voted on a motion to certify the examinations. With one member recused, the CSB deadlocked 2 to 2, resulting in a decision not to certify the results. Explaining his vote to certify the results, Chairman Segaloff stated that "nobody convinced me that we can feel comfortable that, in fact, there's some likelihood that there's going to be an exam designed that's going to be less discriminatory."

The CSB's decision not to certify the examination results led to this lawsuit. The plaintiffs—who are the petitioners here—are 17 white firefighters and 1 Hispanic firefighter who passed the examinations but were denied a chance at promotions when the CSB refused to certify the test results. They include the named plaintiff, Frank Ricci, who addressed the CSB at multiple meetings.

* * *

Petitioners allege that when the CSB refused to certify the captain and lieutenant exam results based on the race of the successful candidates, it discriminated against them in violation of Title VII's disparate-treatment provision. The City counters that its decision was permissible because the tests "appear[ed] to violate Title VII's disparate-impact provisions."

Our analysis begins with this premise: The City's actions would violate the disparate-treatment prohibition of Title VII absent some valid defense. All the evidence demonstrates that the City chose not to certify the examination results because of the statistical disparity based on race—i.e., how minority candidates had performed when compared to white candidates. As the District Court put it, the City rejected the test results because "too many whites and not enough minorities would be promoted were the lists to be certified." Without some other justification, this express, race-based decisionmaking violates Title VII's command that employers cannot take adverse employment actions because of an individual's race.

* * *

We consider, therefore, whether the purpose to avoid disparate-impact liability excuses what otherwise would be prohibited disparate-treatment discrimination. Courts often confront cases in which statutes and principles point in different directions. Our task is to provide guidance to employers and courts for situations when these two prohibitions could be in conflict absent a rule to reconcile them. In providing this guidance our decision must be consistent with the important purpose of Title VII—that the workplace be an environment free of discrimination, where race is not a barrier to opportunity.

* * *

In searching for a standard that strikes a more appropriate balance, we note that this Court has considered cases similar to this one, albeit in the context of the Equal Protection Clause of the Fourteenth Amendment. The Court has held that certain government actions to remedy past racial discrimination—actions that are themselves based on race—are constitutional only where there is a "strong basis in evidence" that the remedial actions were necessary. Richmond v. J. A. Croson Co., 488 U.S. 469, 500 (1989). This suit does not call on us to consider whether the statutory constraints under Title VII must be parallel in all respects to those under the Constitution. That does not mean the constitutional authorities are irrelevant, however. Our cases discussing constitutional principles can provide helpful guidance in this statutory context.

Writing for a plurality in *Wygant* [v. Jackson Bd. of Ed., 476 U.S. 267 (1986)] and announcing the strong-basis-in-evidence standard, Justice Powell recognized the tension between eliminating segregation and discrimination on the one hand and doing away with all governmentally imposed discrimination based on race on the other. The plurality stated that those "related constitutional duties are not always harmonious," and that "reconciling them requires ... employers to act with extraordinary care." The plurality required a strong basis in evidence because "[e]videntiary support for the conclusion that remedial action is warranted becomes crucial when the remedial program is challenged in court by nonminority employees." The Court applied the same standard in *Croson*, observing that "an amorphous claim that there has been past discrimination ... cannot justify the use of an unyielding racial quota."

The same interests are at work in the interplay between the disparate-treatment and disparate-impact provisions of Title VII. Congress has imposed liability on employers for unintentional discrimination in order to rid the workplace of "practices that are fair in form, but discriminatory in operation." But it has also prohibited employers from taking adverse employment actions "because of" race. Applying the strong-basis-in-evidence standard to Title VII gives effect to both the disparate-treatment and disparate-impact provisions, allowing violations of one in the name of compliance with the other only in certain, narrow circumstances. The standard leaves ample room for employers' voluntary compliance efforts, which are essential to the statutory scheme and to Congress's efforts to eradicate workplace discrimination. And the standard appropriately constrains employers' discretion in making race-based decisions: It limits that discretion to cases in which there is a strong basis in evidence of disparate-impact liability, but it is not so restrictive that it allows employers to act only when there is a provable, actual violation.

Resolving the statutory conflict in this way allows the disparate-impact prohibition to work in a manner that is consistent with other provisions of Title VII, including the prohibition on adjusting employment-related test scores on the basis of race. Examinations like those administered by the City create legitimate expectations on the part of those who took the tests. As is the case with any promotion exam, some of the firefighters here invested substantial time, money, and personal commitment in preparing for the tests. Employment tests can be an important part of a neutral selection system that safeguards against the very racial animosities Title VII was intended to prevent. Here, however, the firefighters saw their efforts invalidated by the City in sole reliance upon race-based statistics.

* * *

Title VII does not prohibit an employer from considering, before administering a test or practice, how to design that test or practice in order to provide a fair opportunity for all individuals, regardless of their race. And when, during the test-design stage, an employer invites comments to ensure the test is fair, that process can provide a common ground for open discussions toward that end. We hold only that, under Title VII, before an employer can engage in intentional discrimination for the asserted purpose of avoiding or remedying an unintentional disparate impact, the employer must have a strong basis in evidence to believe it will be subject to disparate-impact liability if it fails to take the race-conscious, discriminatory action.

* * *

The racial adverse impact here was significant, and petitioners do not dispute that the City was faced with a prima facie case of disparate-impact liability. On the captain exam, the pass rate for white candidates was 64 percent but was 37.5 percent for both black and Hispanic candidates. On the lieutenant exam, the pass rate for white candidates was 58.1 percent; for black candidates, 31.6 percent; and for Hispanic candidates, 20 percent. The pass rates of minorities, which were approximately one-half the pass rates for white candidates, fall well below the 80–percent standard set by the EEOC to implement the disparate-impact provision of Title VII. Based on how the passing candidates ranked and an application of the "rule of three," certifying the examinations would have meant that the City could not have considered black candidates for any of the then-vacant lieutenant or captain positions.

Based on the degree of adverse impact reflected in the results, respondents were compelled to take a hard look at the examinations to determine whether certifying the results would have had an impermissible disparate impact. The problem for respondents is that a prima facie case of disparate-impact liability—essentially, a threshold showing of a significant statistical disparity, and nothing more—is far from a strong basis in evidence that the City would have been liable under Title VII had it certified the results.

That is because the City could be liable for disparate-impact discrimination only if the examinations were not job related and consistent with business necessity, or if there existed an equally valid, less-discriminatory alternative that served the City's needs but that the City refused to adopt. We conclude there is no strong basis in evidence to establish that the test was deficient in either of these respects

* * *

The record in this litigation documents a process that, at the outset, had the potential to produce a testing procedure that was true to the promise of Title VII: No individual should face workplace discrimination based on race. Respondents thought about promotion qualifications and relevant experience in neutral ways. They were careful to ensure broad racial participation in the design of the test itself and its administration. As we have discussed at length, the process was open and fair.

The problem, of course, is that after the tests were completed, the raw racial results became the predominant rationale for the City's refusal to certify the results. The injury arises in part from the high, and justified, expectations of the candidates who had participated in the testing process on the terms the City had established for the promotional process. Many of the candidates had studied for months, at considerable personal and financial expense, and thus the injury caused by the City's reliance on raw racial statistics at the end of the process was all the more severe. Confronted with arguments both for and against certifying the test results—and threats of a lawsuit either way—the City was required to make a difficult inquiry. But its hearings produced no strong evidence of a disparate-impact violation, and the City was not entitled to disregard the tests based solely on the racial disparity in the results.

* * *

Petitioners are entitled to summary judgment on their Title VII claim, and we therefore need not decide the underlying constitutional question. The judgment of the Court of Appeals is reversed, and the cases are remanded for further proceedings consistent with this opinion.

* * *

■ JUSTICE SCALIA, concurring.

I join the Court's opinion in full, but write separately to observe that its resolution of this dispute merely postpones the evil day on which the Court will have to confront the question: Whether, or to what extent, are the disparate-impact provisions of Title VII of the Civil Rights Act of 1964 consistent with the Constitution's guarantee of equal protection? The question is not an easy one.

* * *

The Court's resolution of these cases makes it unnecessary to resolve these matters today. But the war between disparate impact and equal protection will be waged sooner or later, and it behooves us to begin thinking about how—and on what terms—to make peace between them.

■ JUSTICE ALITO, with whom JUSTICE SCALIA and JUSTICE THOMAS join, concurring.

* * *

■ JUSTICE GINSBURG, with whom JUSTICE STEVENS, JUSTICE SOUTER, and JUSTICE BREYER join, dissenting.

In assessing claims of race discrimination, "[c]ontext matters." Grutter v. Bollinger, 539 U.S. 306, 327 (2003). In 1972, Congress extended Title VII of the Civil Rights Act of 1964 to cover public employment. At that time, municipal fire departments across the country, including New Haven's, pervasively discriminated against minorities. The extension of Title VII to cover jobs in firefighting effected no overnight change. It took decades of persistent effort, advanced by Title VII litigation, to open firefighting posts to members of racial minorities.

The white firefighters who scored high on New Haven's promotional exams understandably attract this Court's sympathy. But they had no vested right to promotion. Nor have other persons received promotions in preference to them. New Haven maintains that it refused to certify the test results because it believed, for good cause, that it would be vulnerable to a Title VII disparate-impact suit if it relied on those results. The Court today holds that New Haven has not demonstrated "a strong basis in evidence" for its plea. In so holding, the Court pretends that "[t]he City rejected the test results solely because the higher scoring candidates were white." That pretension, essential to the Court's disposition, ignores substantial evidence of multiple flaws in the tests New Haven used. The Court similarly fails to acknowledge the better tests used in other cities, which have yielded less racially skewed outcomes.

By order of this Court, New Haven, a city in which African–Americans and Hispanics account for nearly 60 percent of the population, must today be served—as it was in the days of undisguised discrimination—by a fire department in which members of racial and ethnic minorities are rarely seen in command positions. In arriving at its order, the Court barely acknowledges the pathmarking decision in Griggs v. Duke Power Co., 401 U. S. 424 (1971), which explained the centrality of the disparate-impact concept to effective enforcement of Title VII. The Court's order and opinion, I anticipate, will not have staying power.

* * *

Neither Congress' enactments nor this Court's Title VII precedents (including the now-discredited decision in *Wards Cove* [v. Atonio, 490 U.S. 642 (1989)]) offer even a hint of "conflict" between an employer's obligations under the statute's disparate-treatment and disparate-impact provisions. Standing on an equal footing, these twin pillars of Title VII advance the same objectives: ending workplace discrimination and promoting genuinely equal opportunity.

Yet the Court today sets at odds the statute's core directives. When an employer changes an employment practice in an effort to comply with Title VII's disparate-impact provision, the Court reasons, it acts "because of race"—something Title VII's disparate-treatment provision, generally forbids. This characterization of an employer's compliance-directed action shows little attention to Congress' design or to the *Griggs* line of cases Congress recognized as pathmarking.

* * *

In codifying the *Griggs* and *Albemarle* [Paper Co. v. Moody, 422 U.S. 405 (1975)] instructions, Congress declared unambiguously that selection criteria operating to the disadvantage of minority group members can be retained only if justified by business necessity. In keeping with Congress' design, employers who reject such criteria due to reasonable doubts about their reliability can hardly be held to have engaged in discrimination "because of" race. A reasonable endeavor to comply with the law and to ensure that qualified candidates of all races have a fair opportunity to compete is simply not what Congress meant to interdict. I would therefore hold that an employer who jettisons a selection device when its disproportionate racial impact becomes apparent does not violate Title VII's disparate-treatment bar automatically or at all, subject to this key condition: The employer must have good cause to believe the device would not withstand examination for business necessity.

* * *

Our precedents defining the contours of Title VII's disparate-treatment prohibition further confirm the absence of any intra-statutory discord. In Johnson v. Transportation Agency, Santa Clara Cty., 480 U. S. 616 (1987), we upheld a municipal employer's voluntary affirmative-action plan against a disparate-treatment challenge. Pursuant to the plan, the employer selected a woman for a road-dispatcher position, a job category traditionally regarded as "male." A male applicant who had a slightly higher interview score brought suit under Title VII. This Court rejected his claim and approved the plan, which allowed consideration of gender as "one of numerous factors." Such consideration, we said, is "fully consistent with Title VII" because plans of that order can aid "in eliminating the vestiges of discrimination in the workplace."

This litigation does not involve affirmative action. But if the voluntary affirmative action at issue in *Johnson* does not discriminate within the meaning of Title VII, neither does an employer's reasonable effort to comply with Title VII's disparate-impact provision by refraining from action of doubtful consistency with business necessity.

The Court's decision in this litigation underplays a dominant Title VII theme. This Court has repeatedly emphasized that the statute "should not be read to thwart" efforts at voluntary compliance. Such compliance, we have explained, is "the preferred means of achieving [Title VII's] objectives." The strong-basis-in-evidence standard, however, as barely described in general, and cavalierly applied in this case, makes voluntary compliance a hazardous venture.

As a result of today's decision, an employer who discards a dubious selection process can anticipate costly disparate-treatment litigation in which its chances for success—even for surviving a summary-judgment motion—are highly problematic. Concern about exposure to disparate-impact liability, however well grounded, is insufficient to insulate an employer from attack. Instead, the employer must make a "strong" showing that (1) its selection method was "not job related and consistent with business necessity," or (2) that it refused to adopt "an equally valid, less-discriminatory alternative." It is hard to see how these requirements differ from demanding that an employer establish "a provable, actual violation" *against itself*. There is indeed a sharp conflict here, but it is not the false one the Court describes between Title VII's core provisions. It is, instead, the discordance of the Court's opinion with the voluntary compliance ideal.

* * *

Relying heavily on written tests to select fire officers is a questionable practice, to say the least. Successful fire officers, the City's description of the position makes clear, must have the "[a]bility to lead personnel effectively, maintain discipline, promote harmony, exercise sound judgment, and cooperate with other officials." These qualities are not well measured by written tests. Testifying before the CSB, Christopher Hornick, an exam-design expert with more than two decades of relevant experience, was emphatic on this point: Leadership skills, command presence, and the like "could have been identified and evaluated in a much more appropriate way."

* * *

This case presents an unfortunate situation, one New Haven might well have avoided had it utilized a better selection process in the first place. But what this case does not present is race-based discrimination in violation of Title VII. I dissent from the Court's judgment, which rests on the false premise that respondents showed "a significant statistical disparity," but "nothing more."

QUESTIONS

1. The majority asserted there is a serious conflict between the disparate impact and disparate treatment branches of Title VII doctrine, a point strongly contested by the dissent. Congress specifically approved of the Supreme Court-developed disparate impact doctrine when it enacted the Civil Rights Act of 1991. Does the *Ricci* decision suggest any type of congressional intervention

2. Suppose the City of Old Haven, concerned about possible bias in its promotion examination, received "provisional" test results without any names, but containing a breakdown of scores by race/ethnicity. The examinees received the same results. The city, upon seeing the disparate impact, decides not to use the results because it considers them invalid, not job-related, and unacceptably skewed by race and ethnicity. Concern for potential liability is not a factor. Could the white firefighters prevail in a lawsuit to discover their scores and to require the tests to be used in determining promotions? Can you distinguish *Ricci*?

3. What does *Ricci* portend for the future of *Griggs*? Justice Scalia strongly hints at his view that the disparate impact doctrine is unconstitutional under the Equal Protection clause. Do you agree?

4. Do you agree with Justice Ginsburg's prediction of the short life of the *Ricci* analysis?

5. Consider the difficulties facing an employer seeking to avoid disparate-impact liability stemming from employment tests. On the one hand, the Supreme Court established in *Ricci* that an employer generally may not preemptively abandon test results that seem to exhibit racial skewing. The Court stated that an employer must have a "strong basis in evidence" for suspecting disparate impact before it can invalidate a test, but the Court warned that a "threshold showing of a significant statistical disparity" does not constitute such a basis. On the other hand, the Court suggested in Lewis v. Chicago, 130 S.Ct. 1499 (2010), that racially skewed results such as those in *Ricci* constitute a prima facie showing of disparate impact. In *Lewis*, the plaintiffs argued that a hiring test administered by the Chicago Fire Department disproportionately eliminated minority candidates. The Court found that statistical evidence similar to that in *Ricci* supported a "cognizable claim" of disparate impact. To what extent do the combined holdings of *Ricci* and *Lewis* make it difficult for an employer to forestall a disparate-impact lawsuit?

Page 326.   Please add the following note.

4A. A news station chose not to renew the contract of a white male news anchor and replaced him instead with an African–American male anchor, explaining that they wanted a more friendly, approachable personality for the anchor position. The dismissed anchorman's race discrimination claim failed when the Court of Appeal of California upheld summary judgment for the employer because the plaintiff showed neither racial animus nor pretext. See Hicks v. KNTV TV, 73 Cal.Rptr.3d 240 (Cal. Ct. App. 2008).

E.   DISCRIMINATION BASED ON FACTORS OTHER THAN RACE OR SEX

1.   RELIGION

Page 334.   Please add the following note.

3A. Doyle Ollis, a Protestant, was a sales associate for a homebuilding company. John Smith, the owner of the company, believed in reincarnation and that a person's traumas in past lives can explain his or her behavior in the present. The company required employees to attend sessions of Mind Body Energy (MBE) to cleanse their negative energy. They were also encouraged to read Buddhist and Hindu teachings. Ollis complained to his supervisor and to senior management that these sessions conflicted with his religion and made him uncomfortable. After a complaint of sexual harassment was lodged against him (by a female employee later discharged for removing her clothing at a golf outing and doing cartwheels naked on the golf course), Ollis was fired for "poor leadership and lack of judgment." Ollis brought actions for religious discrimination and retaliatory discharge. The jury found in his favor and awarded him $1 in nominal damages, and the court awarded him attorney fees and costs. The Eighth Circuit affirmed. See Ollis v. HearthStone Homes, Inc., 495 F.3d 570 (8th Cir. 2007).

Page 336.   Please add the following to note 10.

Many of the reasonable accommodation cases continue to grapple with the question of modifying employee work schedules to accommodate religious observances. In general, the courts have held that employers need not accede completely to an employee's requested accommodation, even if doing so would not be an undue hardship, so long as the employer makes a reasonable effort to eliminate the conflict between work and religious practices. See, e.g., EEOC v. Firestone Fibers & Textiles Co., 515 F.3d 307 (4th Cir. 2008) (employee absences); Morrissette–Brown v. Mobile Infirmary Med. Center, 506 F.3d 1317 (11th Cir. 2007) (swapping schedules with other employees).

Page 337.   Please add the following to note 15.

See also LeBoon v. Lancaster Jewish Community Center Ass'n, 503 F.3d 217 (3d Cir. 2007) (non-profit organization with mission "to enhance and promote Jewish life, identity, and continuity" was exempt under Title VII).

Page 337.   Please add the following to note.

16.   Since the mid–1990s, the federal government has supported "faith-based initiatives" to supply federally-funded social services (e.g., substance abuse treatment) through religious-affiliated organizations. These efforts have become known as "Charitable Choice," to emphasize that the recipient has a choice of secular or religious social service providers. See www.whitehouse.gov/government/fbci/guidance/charitable.html. The courts have not ruled on whether the religious groups may use religion as a criterion in hiring employees who provide these services. Title VII case law suggests that the ministerial exception of Title VII would not apply, but the Bush Administration has taken the opposite view. For a general discussion of the ministerial exception, see Note, The Ministerial Exception to Title VII: The Case for a Deferential Primary Duties Test, 121 Harv. L. Rev. 1776 (2008).

2.   National Origin

Page 345.   Please add the following to note 6.

See Montes v. Vail Clinic, Inc., 497 F.3d 1160 (10th Cir. 2007) (upholding hospital's English-only rule which prohibited housekeepers from speaking Spanish for job-related discussions while working in operating room department).

3.   Age

Page 352.   Please add the following note.

4A.   Section 623(d) of the ADEA, the "anti-retaliation" provision, makes it unlawful to discriminate against an individual because the individual "has opposed any practice made unlawful by this section, or because such individual . . . has made a charge, testified, assisted, or participated in any manner in an investigation, proceeding, or litigation under this chapter." In Gomez–Perez v. Potter, 553 U.S. 474 (2008), the Supreme Court held that section 633a(a), which prohibits "discrimination based on age" in federal employment, also prohibits retaliation. The Court held that the absence of an explicit anti-retaliation provision in the federal sector part of the ADEA did not preclude a claim for retaliation.

Page 353.   Please add the following notes.

6A.   Which party should bear the burden of persuasion in establishing "reasonable factors other than age" in a disparate impact claim under the ADEA? In Meacham v. Knolls Atomic Power Laboratory, 552 U.S. 1162 (2008), the Court held that an employer defending a disparate impact claim under the ADEA bears both the burden of production and the burden of persuasion for the RFOA defense. The Court held that the business necessity defense is inapplicable under the ADEA.

6B.   In Gross v. FBL Fin. Servs., 129 S.Ct. 2343 (2009), the Supreme Court, 5–4, held that the mixed motive analysis of Price Waterhouse v. Hopkins (p. 232), as amended by Congress in the Civil Rights Act of 1991 (p. 242), does not apply to age discrimination cases. For ADEA cases, the plaintiff must show that age discrimination was a "but-for" cause of the adverse employment action and not merely a "motivating factor" as is the law for Title VII cases alleging discrimination based on race, color, religion, sex, or national origin.

Page 354.   Please add the following note.

9A.   In Sprint/United Mgmt. Co. v. Mendelsohn, 552 U.S. 379 (2008), the plaintiff sought to support his age discrimination claim by introducing "me, too" evidence testimony by his co-workers that they were also discriminated against on the basis of age by other supervisors. The Supreme Court held that "me, too" evidence is not subject to a per se rule of admissibility under the ADEA. The district court must consider many factors in determining relevance and balancing the probative value against the possible prejudicial effect of the evidence.

4.   DISABILITY

Page 363.   Please add the following to note 3.

In 2007, Maine amended its Human Relations Act to include a list of 27 impairments that are covered regardless of their severity, including cancer, diabetes, epilepsy, heart disease, HIV/AIDS, and mental retardation. Me. Rev. Stat. Ann. § 4553–A. What are the advantages and disadvantages of this approach?

Page 374.   Please add the following to note 8.

Should an employer with a job opening have to give preference to a current employee with a disability who is seeking reassignment? See Huber v. Wal–Mart Stores, Inc., 486 F.3d 480 (8th Cir. 2007), cert. dismissed, 552 U.S. 1136 (2008) (8th Circuit held no; case was settled while pending before the Supreme Court). If an employer has no duty to provide a preference for reassignment, what is the employer's duty?

Page 376.   Please add the following notes.

14.   Plaintiffs have fared very poorly in ADA litigation, losing over 90 percent of the cases prior to 2008. Why? Does that mean that the ADA is unnecessary or a policy failure? See Sharona Hoffman, Settling the Matter: Does Title I of the ADA Work?, 59 Ala. L. Rev. 305 (2008). The number one reason for such a poor record was the narrow judicial interpretations of the definition of "individual with a disability." The ADA Amendments Act of 2008, P.L. 110–325 (2008), was enacted specifically to overrule *Sutton*. According to Congress, "the holdings of the Supreme Court in Sutton v. United Air Lines, Inc., 527 U.S. 471 (1999) and its companion cases have narrowed the broad scope of protection intended to be afforded by the ADA, thus eliminating protection for many individuals whom Congress intended to protect." ADA Amendments Act of 2008, § 2(a)(4). Furthermore, the purposes of the new Act are "to reject the requirement enunciated in Sutton ... and its companion cases that whether an impairment substantially limits a major life activity is to determined with reference to the ameliorative effects of mitigating measures." ADA Amendments Act of 2008, § 2(b)(8).

15.   The ADA Amendments Act of 2008, P.L. 110–325 (2008), was enacted to overrule *Toyota*. According to Congress, "the holding of the Supreme Court in Toyota Motor Mfg., Kentucky, Inc. v. Williams, 534 U.S. 184 (2002), further narrowed the scope of protection intended to be afforded by the ADA; ... as a result ..., lower courts have incorrectly found in individual cases that people with a range of substantially limiting impairments are not people with disabilities; ... in particular, in the case of

Toyota . . ., interpreted the term 'substantially limits' to require a greater degree of limitation than was intended by Congress." ADA Amendments Act of 2008, § 2(a)(5)–(7). In addition, Congress intended "to reject the standards enunciated [in Toyota] that the terms 'substantially' and 'major' in the definition of disability under the ADA 'need to be interpreted strictly to create a demanding standard for qualifying as disabled,'" and to convey that Toyota "has created an inappropriately high level of limitation necessary to obtain coverage under the ADA." ADA Amendments Act of 2008, § 2(b)(4), (5).

ADA AMENDMENTS ACT OF 2008

The ADA Amendments Act of 2008, P.L. 110–325 (2008), was enacted to overturn Supreme Court decisions that narrowly interpreted the definition of an individual with a disability. The essence of the new amendments is captured by the following rule of construction: "The definition of a disability in this Act shall be construed in favor of broad coverage of individuals under this Act, to the maximum extent permitted by the terms of this Act." ADA Amendments Act of 2008, § 3(4)(A). [The Act is reprinted in the Appendix of this supplement.]

Among the major provisions of the 2008 Amendments are the following: (1) the terms "major life activities" and "major bodily functions" are both defined broadly and explicitly; (2) "transitory impairments," which are not covered by the ADA and for which no reasonable accommodations are required, are defined as having an actual or expected duration of six months or less; (3) "episodic conditions" and conditions in remission are covered if they would substantially limit a major life activity when active; (4) impairments are evaluated in their unmitigated state, with the exception of ordinary eyeglasses and contact lenses; (5) the definition of "regarded as having such an impairment" has been expanded significantly and now provides coverage to individuals subjected to an action prohibited by the ADA even if their impairment does not limit a major life activity; and (6) no reasonable accommodation is required for individuals whose coverage is based on the "regarded as" clause.

The courts have uniformly held that the ADA Amendments Act does not apply retroactively to claims pending at the time of its enactment. See, e.g., Lytes v. District of Columbia Water & Sewer Authority, 572 F.3d 936 (D.C. Cir. 2009).

5.   Sexual Orientation

Page 386.   Please add the following to note 7.

The overwhelming weight of authority is that discrimination based on an individual's transgendered status is not prohibited by Title VII's ban on sex discrimination. For example, Etsitty v. Utah Transit Auth., 502 F.3d 1215 (10th Cir. 2007), involved a replacement bus driver without a regular route who used public restrooms along the various routes. The Tenth Circuit held that the plaintiff, a transgendered individual who was in the process of going from male to female, was not covered under the definition of sex and also could not use the *Price Waterhouse* gender stereotyping theory. Even assuming coverage under Title VII, the court held that the employer's concern about potential liability stemming from the plaintiff's use of female restrooms, while still biologically a male, was a legitimate, nondiscriminatory reason.

PART III

TERMS AND CONDITIONS OF EMPLOYMENT

CHAPTER 5

WAGES AND HOURS

A. FEDERAL AND STATE WAGE AND HOUR REGULATION

Page 410. Please add the following note.

4A. Courts disagree about whether the Fair Labor Standards Act requires employers to pay for travel from home to place of work and for visa fees for temporary, seasonal workers (also called "guest workers") coming from other countries to work legally in the U.S. Arriaga v. Florida Pacific Farms, LLC, 305 F.3d 1228 (11th Cir. 2002), held that employers do need to pay visa, immigration, and travel-from-home fees for H–2A workers because those costs are for the benefit of the employer. But see Castellanos–Contreras v. Decatur Hotels, LLC, 576 F.3d 274 (5th Cir. 2009), reaching the opposite conclusion for H–2B workers. The two decisions agreed that employers do not have to reimburse the fees paid by guest workers to Mexican recruiters.

Page 420. Please add the following at the end of note 4.

4A. The Second Circuit confronted the "bluish collar problem" in two recent cases. The court narrowly construed the exemptions from FLSA's overtime-pay requirements against the employers. In Davis v. J.P. Morgan Chase & Co., an underwriter whose job was to evaluate whether to issue loans to individual applicants was found to be outside FLSA's administrative exemption, since his work constituted "production" of loans for the bank. 587 F.3d 529 (2d Cir. 2009). Similarly, the court held in Young v. Cooper Cameron Corp., 586 F.3d 201 (2d Cir. 2009) that a product design specialist was not within the professional exemption from FLSA's overtime-pay provision because the position required no formal advanced education and knowledge required for the job was not customarily acquired by a prolonged course of specialized intellectual instruction.

Page 420.   Please add the following at the end of note 6.

6A.   The Supreme Court addressed this issue in Long Island Care, Ltd. v. Coke, 551 U.S. 158 (2007). The Court confirmed the validity of the FLSA's companionship service exemption, holding that the exemption applies to services rendered in an individual's home by a person employed by a social service agency. The exemption, however, has been strictly limited to domestic services. For example, in Chao v. Gotham Registry, Inc., 514 F.3d 280 (2d Cir. 2008), a temporary staffing agency required nurses to get approval before working overtime at any facility. This proved difficult as the nurses typically did not know when facilities would request overtime. If the nurses worked overtime without approval of the agency, they were paid overtime only if the agency was able to negotiate a premium price from the facility requesting additional nursing care. Most of the time, the agency was not successful. The Second Circuit held that the agency did not satisfy its obligation under the FLSA, regardless of whether the nurse voluntarily agreed to work overtime at the facility's request without permission and regardless of the agency's lack of control over the nurse's decision to accept overtime work. Do you think the burden on the agency is appropriate considering its lack of power to control overtime? On the other hand, didn't Congress enact the FLSA to help people like these nurses receive fair pay for their work?

7.   Are unpaid internships win-win solutions or illegal employment practices violating minimum wage laws? The legal status of unpaid internships turns on the question whether an intern is an employee under the FLSA. The Supreme Court has held that when trainees did not displace any regular employees and the employer received no immediate advantage from the trainees' work, the trainees were not employees under the FLSA, because "the definition 'suffer or permit to work' was obviously not intended to stamp all persons as employees who, without any express or implied compensation agreement, might work for their own advantage on the premises of another." Walling v. Portland Terminal Co. 330 U.S. 148 (1947). The Wage and Hour Division ("WHD") of the Department of Labor has derived a six-factor test from the *Walling* decision. An unpaid internship is illegal under the FLSA unless all six criteria are satisfied: (1) the training, even though it includes actual operation of the facilities of the employer, is similar to that which would be given in a vocational school; (2) the training is for the benefit of the trainee; (3) the trainees do not displace regular employees, but work under close observation; (4) the employer that provides the training derives no immediate advantage from the activities of the trainees and on occasion the employer's operations may actually be impeded; (5) the trainees are not necessarily entitled to a job at the completion of the training period; and (6) the employer and the trainee understand that the trainees are not entitled to wages for the time spent in training. U.S. Wage and Hour Division, Fact Sheet #71: Internship Programs Under The Fair Labor Standard Act, Department of Labor (April 2010) at http://www.dol.gov/whd/regs/compliance/whdfs71.htm. While WHD's interpretation of the FLSA does not bind the courts, it is entitled to deference. If the six-factor test is applied strictly, can you think of an example of a legally unpaid internship? Would employers have enough incentives to keep most of today's internship programs?

Circuit courts are split on the interpretation of the FLSA in the context of internships and trainee programs. The Fifth Circuit deferred to the WHD and strictly applied the six-factor test. See, e.g., Donovan v. American Airlines, Inc., 686 F.2d 267 (5th Cir. 1982). Atkins v. General Motors Corp., 701 F.2d 1124 (5th Cir. 1983). The Tenth Circuit took a "totality of circumstances" approach and held that the determination of whether a trainee was an employee should not turn on the presence or absence of one factor in the equation. See Reich v. Parker Fire Protection District, 992 F.2d 1023 (10th Cir. 1993). The Fourth Circuit rejected WHD's six-factor test and applied its own "primary beneficiary" test– whether the employer or the trainees principally benefited from the work that the trainees did. See, e.g., McLaughlin v. Ensley, 877 F.2d 1207 (4th Cir. 1989). Reich v. Shiloh True Light Church of Christ, 85 F.3d 616 (4th Cir. 1996) (Table). Finally, a district court opinion written by then-judge Sotomayor suggested a mixed approach that combined the six-factor test and the economic realities test. Archie v. Grand Central Partnership, Inc., 997 F.Supp. 504 (S.D.N.Y. 1998). The court held that formerly homeless and jobless participants in an employment program run by non-profit entities were employees of the program, because two important elements in determining the "economic reality" of an employment situation are met– there was an expectation or contemplation of compensation and the employer received an immediate advantage from any work done by the worker.

The lack of consistency in the interpretation of the FLSA in the context of unpaid internship is problematic. The problems are exacerbated by the increasing number of interns each year. The New York Times reported that the percentage of graduating students who have held internships has increased from 17 percent in 1992 to 50 percent in 2008, up to one-half of which are unpaid. Steven Greenhouse, The Unpaid Intern, Legal or Not, N.Y. Times, April 3, 2010, at B1. Unpaid internships provide incentives for employers to use interns to replace regular workers and institutionalizes socioeconomic disparities by limiting participation to students who can afford to forgo wages. For those who are willing to take unpaid internships, the vagueness of internship-related employment laws leaves many interns unprotected by workplace discrimination and harassment. Kathryn A. Edwards & Alexander Hertel–Fernandez, Not–So–Equal protection: Reforming the Regulation of Student Internships, Economic Policy Institute: Policy Memorandum #160 (April 9, 2010).

8. On June 1, 2010, the New York State Senate passed a bill that would require paid holidays, sick days and vacation days for domestic workers, along with overtime wages. It would also require 14 days' notice, or termination pay, before firing a domestic worker. If reconciled with the version already approved by the New York State Assembly and signed by Governor David A. Paterson, the law would be the first in the nation to require new rights for all domestic workers. This Nanny Bill of Rights would affect an estimated 200,000 workers in the metropolitan area: citizen, legal immigrants and illegal immigrants. Russ Buettner, For Nannies, Hope for Workplace Protection, N.Y. Times, June 3, 2010, at A1.

Page 428. Please insert the following case and delete the first paragraph of note 1.

Adair v. Charter County of Wayne

452 F.3d 482 (6th Cir. 2006), cert. denied, 549 U.S. 1279 (2007).

■ SILER, CIRCUIT JUDGE.

Plaintiffs comprise a group of officers employed by the Wayne County Airport Authority and assigned to several specialty units. While off duty, they were required to carry pagers and to remain within a specified geographic area in order to maintain availability during off-duty hours. They filed suit under the Fair Labor Standards Act, seeking overtime compensation for all hours not on duty but during which they carried the pagers. After suit was filed, Airport Authority management requested that officers return their pagers and also eliminated compensatory time in favor of overtime and assigned county-owned vehicles to the K–9 officers. Based on these actions, Plaintiffs amended their complaint to include claims of retaliation in violation of the FLSA and 42 U.S.C. § 1983. The district court granted summary judgment to Defendants on all claims. Because Plaintiffs are not entitled to overtime pay under the FLSA, and because Defendants' actions do not constitute retaliation, we affirm.

Plaintiffs are police officers assigned to the Wayne County, Michigan airport, which services much of Michigan's lower peninsula, including the entire Detroit metropolitan area. All employees of the airport police department were originally employees of the Wayne County Sheriff's Department until the Airport Authority was formed as a separate entity to operate the airport on March 26, 2002. Generally, Plaintiffs were scheduled to work a forty-hour workweek. If Plaintiffs wanted to work overtime, they would place their names on an overtime list and would be called to work according to seniority and/or their collective bargaining agreement, if and when overtime hours became available. An officer could refuse the overtime offered. Officers working overtime were paid overtime pay.

The Plaintiffs in this case are members of four specialty police units, including the Special Response Unit (SRU–SWAT), Explosive and Ordnance Disposal (EOD–Bomb Squad), K–9, and the Accident Investigation Unit (AI). Officers belonging to these specialty units receive extra "specialty pay." All officers in the four specialty units had to live within a close geographical area to the airport. Members of the K–9 and EOD–Bomb Squad units had to agree, as a condition of employment, to live within a thirty-minute travel time from the airport. SRU/SWAT officers are required to maintain reasonable availability when off duty.

Further, officers assigned to the four specialty units were required to carry digital pagers which operated on a state-wide basis. The pagers were to be carried both on and off duty and always turned on. K–9, SRU–SWAT, and EOD–Bomb Squad officers all agreed to respond to calls for service at all hours as a condition of being selected to the unit. Two Plaintiffs testified that they were orally counseled for not responding when paged, and other Plaintiffs testified they understood that failure to respond to an off-duty page would result in discipline.

Prior to September 11, 2001, Plaintiffs claim they generally could attend to their personal business while off duty, subject to responding when paged. However, immediately after the events of September 11, the officers were placed on twelve-hour shifts, seven days per week, and had their leave and vacation days cancelled. On September 21, the shifts were reduced to ten hours, six days per week. SRU–SWAT, K–9, and EOD–Bomb Squad officers were told that, when they were off duty, they had to stay close to home and be able to respond immediately should the need arise. This continued until November 26, 2001, when the officers went on a five-day per week schedule, ten hours per day, and were allowed to use their vacation time.

In October 2001, shortly after the terrorist attacks, Defendant Mark DeBeau was hired as the Director of Public Safety at the airport. He was directed to review his department's administrative functions and expenses. Due to his review, the airport considered a number of changes in its policing operations. Several of these policy changes were later implemented. Airport management issued specially-outfitted sports utility vehicles to each of its K–9 officers, and discontinued the payment of flat rate mileage for driving to and from work to those officers. Management also decided to freeze the accumulation and use of banked compensatory time, or "comp time," due to staffing problems caused by the September 11 terrorist attacks and resulting personnel requirements mandated by the federal government. Allowing officers to utilize comp time, in addition to vacation time, forced the airport to rely on (and pay for) overtime to compensate for their absences. Instead of paying officers comp time for certain activities, the airport decided that it would be less costly to pay its officers actual overtime pay. Later, the sport utility vehicles were returned to the airport and the flat rate mileage reimbursement policy was reinstated due to the dissatisfaction of the K–9 unit officers and their union.

In 2002, twenty-five officers filed suit against Wayne County seeking overtime pay under the FLSA. After the initial complaint was filed, airport management collected the pagers from all of its officers at the airport. Plaintiffs then amended their complaint to add a second count under 42 U.S.C. § 1983, alleging that the collection of all pagers was unlawful retaliation against them. Plaintiffs later added a retaliation claim under the FLSA for the changes implemented by the airport as recommended by Mark DeBeau. This appeal names Wayne County and the Wayne County Airport Authority as municipal defendants and DeBeau, Director of Public Safety, as a defendant individually and in his official capacity.

* * *

Plaintiffs first claim that the district court erred in ruling that they failed to state a claim under the FLSA for overtime compensation. Their chief contention is that carrying pagers as required by the airport entitles them to overtime pay for all hours not at work that the pagers were worn.

* * *

Plaintiffs proffer three reasons why the airport management's on-call policy is so "severely restrictive" as to require payment of overtime compensation under the FLSA. First, they argue that their personal pursuits are severely restricted because they are subject to discipline for not responding when paged.

* * *

The district court concluded that Plaintiffs were not severely restricted by the Defendants' on-call policy because Plaintiffs admitted that they could engage in all of their regular activities while off duty. Although Plaintiffs assert that the fear of imposition of discipline alone is sufficient to transform otherwise non-compensable time into compensable time, they provide no precedent holding the same. The on-call policy at issue in this case presents no objective restrictions on Plaintiffs' off-duty time besides requiring them to carry pagers. The law in this circuit plainly states the test for determining whether off-duty time is compensable: whether, during that time, the employer imposes burdens on the employee so onerous that they prevent employees from effectively using their time for personal pursuits. The mere threat of discipline does not, by itself, prevent employees from effectively using their off-duty time for personal pursuits.

* * *

Second, they argue that the restriction on their ability to live outside the geographical limits associated with their positions constitutes severe restriction. However, employment of EOD–Bomb Squad and K–9 officers was contingent on their agreement to live within thirty minutes of the airport. The pagers they carried operated on a state-wide basis, allowing them to travel throughout Michigan in their off-duty time. Plaintiffs could refuse to answer pages. If they did report to work when paged, they received overtime pay for such work. Importantly, Plaintiffs admitted that they could engage in all of their regular personal activities while off duty. Additionally, Plaintiffs failed to demonstrate that they received so many calls that they could not effectively use their off-duty time. In three years, SRU–SWAT was called only once, while EOD–Bomb Squad and AI units were called in twice. The K–9 unit was called between fifteen to twenty times.

Third, Plaintiffs argue that the airport's requirement that they remain at home to wait for a call after the September 11, 2001 attacks also severely restricted their ability to attend to personal pursuits. The airport management's post-September 11 terrorist attack policy that temporarily required Plaintiffs to remain close to home for enhanced availability in case of emergency also does not create compensable time. While at home, Plaintiffs' activities were not restricted in any way; thus, the emergency management policy in place during those months did not severely restrict Plaintiffs' personal activities. Moreover, Plaintiffs testified that they were rarely called in during this period. The evidence reveals that Plaintiffs' off-duty time was not utilized predominantly for the employer's benefit, but for the employees'.

* * *

Plaintiffs argue that the district court erred in finding that they failed to state a claim of retaliation in violation of the FLSA. They specifically disagree with the district court's conclusion that the actions taken by airport management were not materially adverse and were not motivated by the filing of Plaintiffs' lawsuit.

The anti-retaliation provision of FLSA provides that an employer is prohibited from "discharg[ing] or in any other manner discriminat[ing] against [an] employee because such employee has filed [a] complaint or instituted . . . any proceeding under [the FLSA]." To establish a prima facie case of retaliation, an employee must prove that (1) he or she engaged in a protected activity under the FLSA; (2) his or her exercise of this right was known by the employer; (3) thereafter, the employer took an employment action adverse to her; and (4) there was a causal connection between the protected activity and the adverse employment action.

Plaintiffs here satisfy the first two prongs of the burden-shifting analysis. They engaged in a FLSA-protected activity, filing a cause of action seeking overtime pay, and notified Defendants of the activity by serving them with the complaint. More questionable is whether Plaintiffs satisfied the third and fourth prongs of the framework.

The third prong requires an adverse employment action taken against the employee by the employer. The employment action must be materially adverse. Employment actions qualifying as materially adverse include "termination of employment, a demotion evidenced by a decrease in wage or salary, a less distinguished title, a material loss of benefits, significantly diminished material responsibilities, or other indices that might be unique to a particular situation." Mere inconvenience or an alteration of job responsibilities fail to constitute materially adverse employment actions.

Plaintiffs complain that Defendants took adverse action against them by ordering their pagers returned. Such an action is not materially adverse. Plaintiffs did not suffer any loss or diminution of wages, benefits, or responsibilities. Moreover, Plaintiffs' initial action solely concerned their dissatisfaction with carrying the pagers; they cannot now credibly assert that management's decision to remove the pagers was in any way adverse.

Plaintiffs also complain that Defendants' decision to eliminate the mileage reimbursement for K–9 officers and to provide them with county-owned and maintained SUVs, specially outfitted with necessary equipment for the officers' dogs, for transportation was materially adverse. Plaintiffs were not denied any reimbursement for mileage already accrued on their personal vehicles; Defendants only changed the policy for K–9 transportation, and the evidence reflects that the policy change was not taken to retaliate against the Plaintiffs. Indeed, the purchase of the SUVs was a subject of negotiations for several years prior to May 2002 and two weeks after the SUVs were issued to the officers, they were returned to the county and the mileage reimbursement was reinstated. The transportation policy change did not constitute an adverse employment action.

Plaintiffs finally complain that the freeze on accumulation and use of banked compensatory time was an adverse action. This did not result in a material loss of benefits, termination, demotion, transfer, or alteration of job responsibilities. Plaintiffs simply were required to utilize vacation days for just that—vacation—rather than permitted to save vacation time and later exchange it for pay. Moreover, the Airport Authority did not deprive Plaintiffs of any benefit by freezing the accumulation of overtime pay; now officers working overtime receive pay instead of earning comp time. Plaintiffs fail to prove that the actions taken by the Airport Authority were materially adverse.

The fourth prong of the prima facie case requires Plaintiffs to prove a causal connection, that is, that the filing of the suit caused the alleged retaliation. In order to demonstrate a causal connection, "a plaintiff must produce sufficient evidence from which an inference can be drawn that the adverse action would not have been taken had the plaintiff not filed a discrimination action."

* * *

Although Plaintiffs here speculate that the Airport Authority implemented policy changes to retaliate against them for filing suit, they provide no factual support for their contentions. Subjective beliefs, without affirmative evidence, are insufficient to establish a claim of retaliation. That the changes occurred does not compel the conclusion that they occurred to retaliate against the Plaintiffs. Moreover, that changes were imposed on officers not involved in the lawsuit strongly negates the argument that airport management's actions were motivated by the filing of the suit.

* * *

Plaintiffs' final claim charges Defendants with violating their First Amendment right to be free from retaliation for speaking out against official policy and for filing a lawsuit. The district court properly found that Plaintiffs failed to state a claim for relief under Section 1983.

To state a successful claim under 42 U.S.C. § 1983, Plaintiffs "must identify a right secured by the United States Constitution and the deprivation of that right by a person acting under color of state law." Plaintiffs need to demonstrate that (1) the conduct at issue must have been under color of state law, (2) the conduct caused a deprivation of constitutional rights, and (3) the deprivation occurred without due process of law. Because Section 1983 is not itself a source of substantive rights, but only a method for vindicating federal rights elsewhere conferred, a plaintiff must set forth specific constitutional grounds for asserting a Section 1983 claim.

* * *

Plaintiffs here, public employees, fail to demonstrate that their speech touched on matters of public concern. They cite one newspaper article and one editorial in the Detroit News that demanded return of the pagers to Plaintiffs in order to ensure the safety of Michigan residents traveling through the airport. The article and editorial, however, were published after the fact of the lawsuit's filing, which initially contained only complaints about the Plaintiffs' concerns regarding non-payment of overtime while on call. Nothing in the FLSA claim indicates that Plaintiffs were filing a lawsuit involving matters of public concern. Thus Plaintiffs establish no First Amendment Free Speech Clause claim. Nor do they establish a First Amendment Petition Clause claim, citing no authority to illustrate that public employees enjoy the right to file lawsuits to redress grievances without commenting on matters of public concern.

AFFIRMED.

Page 429. Please add the following note.

3A. New York City fire alarm inspectors go directly from home to the places they will inspect and return home at the end of the workday. Thus they must pick up inspection documents on Friday at the office and carry them back and forth from home to their inspection locations. Held: The city need not pay the inspectors for their commuting time, although they must bring documents with them. The instructors had argued that commuting sometimes took longer because carrying a briefcase caused them to miss a train or bus. Singh v. City of New York, 524 F.3d 361 (2d Cir. 2008).

Page 430.   Please add the following after note 6.

6A.   The Ninth Circuit has held that when an employer changes its shift schedule to accommodate its employees' scheduling desires, the mere fact that pay rates changed, altering the old and new scheduling schemes in an attempt to keep overall pay revenue-neutral, does not violate the FSLA's overtime pay requirements. Parth v. Pomona Valley Hospital, 584 F.3d 794 (9th Cir. 2009). In response to the nurses' request, the Pomona Valley Hospital Medical Center ("PVHMC") developed and implemented an optional 12–hour shift schedule and pay plan that provided nurses the option of working a 12–hour shift schedule in exchange for receiving a lower base hourly salary and time-and-a-half pay for hours worked in excess of eight per day. Many nurses opted to work the 12–hour shift because it provides them more scheduling flexibility and allows them to spend less time commuting to work. As a result, nurses who volunteered for the 12–hour shift schedule would make approximately the same amount of money as they made on the 8–hour shift schedule while working the same number of hours. Are the base hourly pay rate differences between the 8–hour and 12–hour shifts justified, considering that nurses working both shifts perform the same job duties? Is the 12–hour base pay rate an unlawful "artifice" designed to avoid the FLSA's overtime and maximum hours requirements?

Page 430.   Please add the following note.

8.   Are Department of Justice attorneys entitled to overtime pay? In Doe v. United States, 463 F.3d 1314 (Fed. Cir. 2006), cert. denied, 549 U.S. 1321 (2007), plaintiff John Doe and a class of similarly situated attorneys brought a claim for administratively uncontrollable overtime (AUO) pay under the Federal Employees Pay Act of 1945. The court ruled against the unhappy attorneys, holding that "attorney" was not one of the limited positions subject to overtime compensation under the act.

B.   WHAT IS A JOB WORTH?

Page 465.   Please add the following note.

9.   When the House of Representatives approved the Ledbetter amendment, see supplement p. 42, it separately approved H.R. 11, the Paycheck Fairness Act. As of July 1, 2009, the Senate had not considered the Paycheck Fairness Act. Among other provisions, the House-approved Paycheck Fairness Act would amend the Equal Pay Act to:

> (1) replace the EPA's exemption for wage rate differentials "based on any other factor other than sex" with an exemption only for "bona fide factors, such as education, training or experience";

(2) limit the bona fide factor defense to employer demonstrations that the factor is not derived from a sex-based differential, is job-related with respect to the position in question, and is consistent with business necessity; in addition, the employee would be able to show that an alternative employment practice would serve the same business purpose without producing a gendered differential in pay;

(3) prohibit retaliation against employees who inquire about, discuss, or disclose wages with other workers as part of a sex discrimination inquiry.

CHAPTER 6

HEALTH BENEFITS

A. INTRODUCTION
HEALTH CARE REFORM AND EMPLOYMENT

Two contentious and complicated laws were enacted in early 2010 to reform the American health care system. On March 30, 2010, President Barack Obama signed the Health Care and Education Reconciliation Act, P.L. 111–152, also known as the "Reconciliation Act," making changes to the Patient Protection and Affordable Care Act, P.L. 111–148, also known as "PPACA" and the "Affordable Care Act," passed one week earlier. The Acts collectively make numerous changes to existing laws and add a variety of new programs in an effort to expand access to health care, improve quality, prohibit discriminatory practices by insurers, and reduce costs. The legislation was designed to augment rather than supplant employer-based group health plans, and in several ways the new laws attempt to promote and support the role of employers in health care finance.

The comprehensive set of reforms creates obligations on employers and employees. Besides offering tax credits and imposing penalties on employers, the new legislation establishes a mandate on individuals to purchase health insurance. It also reforms health insurance plans in general, affecting private employer-sponsored health plans, currently estimated as covering 176 million Americans nation-wide.

Congressional findings show that national health spending in 2009 was $2.5 trillion, or 17.6% of the economy, and it is expected to increase in the next ten years to $4.7 trillion. According to the U.S. Census Bureau, the number of Americans that were uninsured in 2008 was 46.3 million, up from 45.7 million in 2007 and comprising 15.4% of the population. The Congressional Budget Office estimates that both pieces of legislation would produce a net reduction in federal deficits of $124 billion from 2010 to 2019 as a result of changes deriving from health care and revenue provisions.

Furthermore, the new law projected to cover an additional 32 million Americans and increase the number Americans who are insured to reach near-universal coverage in the U.S.

Despite these optimistic projections, the new health care reform legislation has been met with heated opposition and strong criticism. Pending constitutional litigation and pledges by some lawmakers to repeal some or all of the law overshadow the phased implementation of the various provisions.

EMPLOYER RESPONSIBILITIES

The Acts impose numerous mandates but also provide a number of benefits to employers based on their size and compensation rates for employees.

Small Business Tax Credit. The laws give incentives to small employers to provide their employees with health coverage; not by imposing penalties, as it does with large employers, but by offering them a tax credit. Section 1421 of the PPACA amends the Internal Revenue Code (IRC) to give small employers a credit for offering their employees health insurance coverage and making contributions towards their coverage beginning in tax year 2010 through 2013. According to the PPACA, a "small employer" is generally defined as an employer with at least one but no more than 100 employees. To be eligible for the tax credit, the employer must have no more than 25 full-time equivalent employees (FTEs). For example, an employer with fewer than 50 half-time workers may be eligible. The employer must also pay an average of $50,000 or less per FTE during each tax year, and pay at least 50% of the premium cost. Small employers would be eligible to receive up to 35% of the employer's contributions towards the premium cost (or 25% for tax-exempt employers). Beginning in 2014, the employer may be eligible to receive a tax credit of up to 50% of the employer's contributions towards the premium cost. However, to be eligible for the full credit the employer must have 10 or fewer FTEs or pay an average of $25,000 or less per FTE. The credit phases out for employers that have more FTEs (10 to 25) or higher wages (an average of between $25,000 to $50,000).

Large Employer Penalty. Under the new laws, employers are not required to provide health insurance coverage; however, beginning in 2014, certain large employers that do not offer health insurance to their employees will be penalized. The PPACA generally defines a "large employer" as an employer that employs an average of 101 employees. Section 1513 of the PPACA provides that "applicable large employers" that do not offer minimum essential health coverage under an eligible employer-sponsored plan, and that have at least one full-time employee who enrolls in a plan on the state health exchange using a federal premium tax credit or cost-sharing reduction, will be liable for a penalty. This penalty is also known as the "play-or-pay" mandate and the "free rider penalty." PPACA § 1513 imposes a penalty in the amount of $2,000 on large employers that do not offer minimum essential health coverage each year (or $166.67 for each month the employer does not provide a plan), multiplied by the number of full-time employees. The first 30 employees do not count towards the penalty.

An "applicable large employer" is defined as an employer with at least 50 full-time employees on business days during the preceding calendar year. A "full-time employee" is defined as an employee who works an average of at least 30 hours per week. "Essential health benefits" includes the following non-comprehensive list of features:

(A) Ambulatory patient services;

(B) Emergency services;

(C) Hospitalization;

(D) Maternity and newborn care;

(E) Mental health and substance use disorder services, including behavioral health treatment;

(F) Prescription drugs;

(G) Rehabilitative and habilitative services and devices;

(H) Laboratory services;

(I) Preventive and wellness services and chronic disease management; and

(J) Pediatric services, including oral and vision care.

Furthermore, large employers that offer coverage described above but whose coverage is not "affordable" or whose coverage does not provide a certain value must pay an additional penalty. To be "affordable" the premium of the employer-sponsored plan must cost less than 9.5% of the employee's household income. The plan must also provide a minimum value of at least 60% of the coverage (i.e., the employer's share must constitute 60% of the employee's covered medical expenses). If the large employer does not meet either of these minimum requirements of coverage, the employer will be liable for a penalty in the amount of $3,000 per year for each full-time employee (or $250 each month that the employer offers coverage below these levels). PPACA § 1513(c)(2) provides a limitation on this penalty, which cannot exceed $2,000 per full-time employee per year (or $166.67 for each month), and the first 30 employees will not count towards the penalty.

Exempt from these penalties are large employers with seasonal workers and large employers that have over 50 full-time employees for only 120 days or less out of the calendar year, and the employees in excess of the 50 employees during that 120–day period are seasonal workers. A "seasonal worker" is defined as a "worker who performs labor or services on a seasonal basis as defined by the Secretary of Labor," and retail workers employed exclusively during holiday seasons.

PPACA § 1514 imposes a number of reporting requirements on large employers falling within the ambit of PPACA § 1513. Large employers must certify on their tax return whether they offer their employees the opportunity to enroll in minimum essential coverage under an eligible employer-sponsored plan. Large employers must also report, among other things, the following: the length of any waiting period; the lowest monthly premium of each enrollment category that the employer-sponsored plan offers; the employer's share of the total costs of benefits under the plan; and the names and numbers of full-time employees receiving coverage under the employer-sponsored plan.

General Reporting Requirement. Beginning in 2011, employers are required to disclose the cost of employer-sponsored coverage on an employee's W–2 annually. Contributions to an FSA are not included in this disclosure requirement.

Automatic Enrollment. The PPACA amended the Fair Labor Standards Act (FLSA) to impose another duty on larger employers. Larger employers that have more than 200 full-time employees and offer group health plans are required to enroll automatically new full-time employees in a health benefits plan. They are also required to continue the enrollment of current employees. These employers must provide adequate notice to their employees of the automatic enrollment program, along with an opportunity for the employee to opt out of the program. Employees must affirmatively opt out of the program if they do not want coverage under their employer. The relevant provision is silent regarding the effective date of this mandate, but most experts have interpreted the provision to be effective in 2014.

Free Choice Vouchers. Beginning in 2014, employers that offer minimum essential coverage through an eligible employer-sponsored plan and pay a portion of the costs will be required to provide "qualified employees" with a "free choice voucher." A free choice voucher can be used by an employee to purchase a qualified health plan on the state health exchange in lieu of receiving coverage through the employer-sponsored plan. A "qualified employee" is defined as an employee: (1) whose required contribution for minimum essential coverage through an eligible employer-sponsored plan is between 8% and 9.8% of his or her household income for the year; (2) whose household income is not greater than 400 percent of the federal poverty line for a similarly-sized family; and (3) who chooses not to participate in a health plan offered by the employer.

The amount of the voucher is the monthly cost the employer would have paid if the employee enrolled in the employer's plan. If the employer offers multiple plans, it would be the plan for which the employer pays the largest portion each month. If this monthly amount exceeds the premium cost of the health plan the employee is enrolled in through the state exchange, the excess funds will be paid to the employee. The voucher is tax-free for employees and it is deductible for employers. Employers may not discriminate against employees who opt to receive free choice vouchers.

Flexible Spending Arrangements (FSAs). Employer contributions to flexible spending arrangements are capped at $2,500 (effective 2013).

Wellness Programs. The new law codifies Health Insurance Portability and Accountability Act (HIPAA) and Employee Retirement Income Security Act (ERISA) regulations regarding employer-sponsored wellness programs. Prior to PPACA and the Reconciliation Act, HIPAA and ERISA had nondiscrimination provisions allowing an exception for employer-sponsored plans that varied benefits, premiums, or contributions based on whether an individual has met standards of wellness programs. Employers were allowed to offer rewards to employees for participating in wellness programs. Subsequently, federal regulatory agencies issued further rules regarding these rewards, including a limit on the incentives that employers could offer employees for participating in the program to 20% of the cost of the plan. PPACA increases the amount of financial incentives that employers can offer employees to 30%. These wellness programs are designed to promote health and prevent illness. The Secretaries of the Department of Health and Human Services (HHS), Department of Labor, and Department of the Treasury may increase the reward to 50% of the cost of coverage if they determine that such an increase is appropriate and is not a "subterfuge for discriminating based on a health status factor," or the reward is not punitive in nature.

Section 10408 of PPACA also allows the HHS Secretary to award grants to small employers to establish a comprehensive workplace wellness program where none exists. To be eligible, the employer must employ fewer than 100 employees who work 25 hours or more per week.

Break Time for Nursing Mothers. The PPACA amends the FLSA by adding a section providing for a reasonable break time for employees to express, or pump breast milk. An employer must also provide a place "other than a bathroom, that is shielded from view and free from intrusion from coworkers and the public" for the employee to express breast milk. This section does not preempt state laws that provide more generous break time laws for nursing mothers. There are some limitations to this provision; for example, contrary to the general FLSA requirement that employers must compensate an employee for breaks that last less than 20 minutes, under this provision employers are not required to compensate an employee for this break time. Moreover, small employers with fewer than 50 employees are not required to comply with this provision if it would impose "undue hardship."

Early Retiree Reinsurance Program. A temporary reinsurance program will be established to reimburse employers for a portion of the cost of providing health insurance coverage to early retirees between the ages of 55 and 64. Employers will receive reimbursement in the amount of 80% of the cost per enrollee over $15,000 and under $90,000. The program will be financed by a $5 billion appropriation from the Department of Treasury and will be effective 90 days after enactment until 2014, or if the HHS Secretary decides to end the program earlier if funds are exhausted.

Medicare Part D Deduction. Medicare Part D was created in 2003 (effective 2006) to provide a subsidy to employers for the costs of prescription drugs for Medicare beneficiaries. PPACA § 9012 eliminates the deduction given to employers for its retiree prescription drug costs including those allocated under the subsidy (effective 2013).

Medicare Part D "Doughnut Hole Fix." Reconciliation Act § 1101 gradually reduces the Medicare Part D "doughnut hole" so that it is fully closed by 2020. It provides a $250 rebate for Medicare Part D enrollees who "hit" the doughnut hole, or reach the threshold in which they must pay for prescription drugs out of pocket, in 2010. The Reconciliation Act also gives a 50% discount on brand name drugs to Part D enrollees in 2011 and a 75% discount by 2020.

Reimbursement for Over-the-Counter Medicines. Effective 2011, employees can only claim reimbursement for prescription drugs and insulin through a Health Savings Account (HSA) or FSA. Therefore, employers will no longer be able to deduct the costs of over-the-counter medicine.

Simple Cafeteria Plan for Small Businesses. PPACA § 9022 adds a simple new cafeteria plan for small businesses (effective 2011).

GENERAL HEALTH REFORMS

The Patient Protection and Affordable Care Act, as modified by the Reconciliation Act, gradually institutes a number of reforms over the next eight years applicable to insurers offering both individual and group health plans. A number of these reforms also apply to "grandfathered health plans," that existed at the time of enactment, or that existed as of March 23, 2010. Grandfathered plans include plans of family members of current enrollees and new employees who enroll subsequent to the time of enactment. These existing plans are grandfathered from many of the PPACA reforms, except for a handful of significant provisions.

Individual and group health plans, including grandfathered plans, are required to comply with the following selected key reforms:

Lifetime and Annual Limits. There is a prohibition on lifetime limits on the dollar value of benefits, and annual limits may only be restricted to the dollar value of "essential health benefits" (effective six months after enactment, or September 23, 2010). Beginning in 2014, annual limits are prohibited altogether.

Rescissions. There is a prohibition on rescissions of coverage for enrollees once they are covered except in cases where the current enrollee has committed fraud or made an intentional misrepresentation of material fact as prohibited by the terms of the plan or coverage (effective six months after enactment).

Coverage of Dependents. Individual and group health plans that provide coverage to dependents must continue to make coverage available to adult dependents up to age 26, regardless of marriage status (effective six months after enactment).

Coverage of Individuals with Preexisting Conditions. The Public Health Service Act (PHSA) is amended to prohibit exclusions with respect to children up to age 18 with preexisting conditions (effective six months after enactment). The prohibition with respect to preexisting conditions will be extended to adults beginning in 2014. In order to assist adults with preexisting conditions until 2014, effective 90 days after enactment (or June 21, 2010) until January 1, 2014, HHS is required to establish a temporary high risk health insurance pool to provide coverage to eligible individuals with a preexisting condition. Individuals are eligible if they are lawfully present in the United States, uninsured, and possess a preexisting condition as defined by the HHS Secretary.

Waiting Periods. There is a prohibition on waiting periods exceeding 90 days (effective 2014).

Individual and group health plans, not including grandfathered plans, are required to comply with the following additional selected reforms:

Preventive Health Services. There is a prohibition on cost-sharing for the following preventive services, including: services rated A or B by the U.S. Preventive Services Task Force; certain recommended immunizations; preventive care for infants, children, and adolescents; and additional preventive care for women such as breast cancer screenings (effective six months after enactment).

Emergency Services. Prior authorizations are not required for emergency services, and emergency services will also be provided regardless of whether the provider is in or out of the plan network (effective six months after enactment).

Clinical Trials. Treatment to individuals participating in clinical trials must be covered (effective 2014). The new law offers tax credits to employers for investment into new therapies to treat areas of unmet medical need, to prevent, detect, or treat chronic or acute diseases and conditions including cancer. Employers must have 250 employees or fewer to qualify for these tax credits, which would cover costs equal to 50% of investments made in 2009 and 2010.

Premium Increases. PPACA amends the Public Health Service Act to require insurers to justify unreasonable increases in premiums for health insurance coverage, prior to implementation of the increase, in an annual state review process, beginning with the plan year 2010. Beginning in 2014, plans with unreasonable premium increases may be prohibited from participating in the state health exchanges.

Appeals Process. An internal and external appeals process must be established for appeals of coverage determinations and claims. The plan must allow an enrollee to review his or her file, present evidence and testimony, and receive continued coverage pending the outcome of the appeals process. Notice of the available internal and external processes must be given to enrollees (effective six months after enactment). The internal process and external process both must meet requirements under certain state and/or federal law, and both processes must be updated with any new standards published by the Secretary of HHS.

Nondiscrimination. The PPACA has a number of provisions designed to prohibit discrimination, shaping rules ranging from enrollment eligibility to marketing. Insurers are prohibited from having eligibility rules for enrollment based on health status, medical condition (including physical or mental illnesses) or medical history, claims experience, receipt of health care, genetic information, disability, evidence of insurability, or any factor determined appropriate by HHS (effective 2014). In addition, there is a prohibition on eligibility rules based on wages, or rules that otherwise have the effect of discriminating in favor of higher wage employees (effective six months after enactment). Insurers are also prohibited from utilizing discriminatory premium rates. Premium rates may only vary based only on the following factors: family composition, age, tobacco use, and geographic area. No rating variation is allowed based on health, race, or gender (effective 2014). Insurers may not employ marketing practices that have the effect of discouraging enrollment by individuals with significant health needs.

INDIVIDUAL RESPONSIBILITY

Concurrent with the employer's obligations under the Patient Protection and Affordable Care Act and the Reconciliation Act, beginning in 2014, individuals will be required to maintain minimal essential health care coverage for themselves and their dependents. Individuals who fail to maintain such coverage will be subject to a penalty to be included in their tax return. The penalty will be either a percentage of the individual's household income, or a flat dollar amount for each year the individual fails to maintain coverage, whichever is greater. The minimum penalty gradually increases each year, and will be (1) 1.0% of the individual's income or $95 in 2014; (2) 2.0% of the individual's income or $325 in 2015; and (3) 2.5% of the individual's income or $625 in 2016, after which the dollar amount will be indexed for inflation.

The new law exempts certain individuals from coverage, including individuals who object to health care coverage on religious grounds, who are not lawfully present in the United States, and who are incarcerated. The new law also provides exceptions from the penalty for certain low-income individuals, including individuals who cannot afford coverage (defined as individuals whose required contribution for coverage would exceed 8% of household income for the taxable year) and individuals whose income is less than 100% of the federal poverty line, members of Indian tribes, and individuals who suffer hardship.

The individual mandate is satisfied by enrollment in eligible employer group health plans, grandfathered plans, government-sponsored plans, such as Medicare and Medicaid, and plans offered in the individual market.

STATE HEALTH EXCHANGES

By January 1, 2014, states are required to establish an "American Health Benefit Exchange" or state health exchange, where individuals who do not have coverage under their employer can purchase qualified health plans. States are also required to establish a Small Business Health Options Program, or "SHOP Exchange," to assist small employers in enrolling their employees in qualified health plans. The state may establish only one exchange to serve both individuals and small employers; moreover, states may establish subsidiary exchanges for different geographical regions, and more than one state can coordinate to establish an interstate health exchange with the approval of the Secretary of HHS. The exchange will facilitate the purchase of health coverage by providing a website where individuals and small employers can compare different plans, which are assigned ratings by the exchange.

The state health exchange must be a government agency or nonprofit entity established by the state. Only qualified health plans may be offered in the exchange. "Small employers" eligible to enroll in the exchange are those employers with 100 or fewer employees, but states may limit participation to employers with 50 or fewer employees for plan years beginning before January 1, 2016. Note that prior to the establishment of the exchange, between 2010 and 2013, only those small employers with 25 or fewer employees are eligible for the small business tax credit under section 1421, indicating that the criteria for small employers under different provisions may differ. Beginning in 2017, states may open up the exchange to large employers.

The exchanges will be funded through grants from the Secretary of HHS to each state, but starting January 1, 2015, the exchange must be self-sustaining. The exchange may charge assessments or user fees to participating insurance companies, or generate funding through other means to support its operations. Note that the exchanges will impose a large financial burden on the state starting in 2015, which may in turn be passed on to individuals. The Office of Personnel Management (OPM) will contract with insurance companies to offer at least two national or multi-state plans in each state's exchange.

FINANCING

In order to raise revenue for the high costs of the new healthcare reforms, the PPACA has a number of revenue offset provisions, including but not limited to the following:

Excise Tax on High Cost Health Coverage. Effective 2018, PPACA § 9001 imposes a 40% excise tax on any "excess benefit" of employer-sponsored high cost health plans, also known as "Cadillac plans." Excess benefits are amounts in excess of certain thresholds set out by the Act, namely health plans that cost more than $10,200 for individuals and more than $27,500 for families. The excise tax does not apply to stand-alone dental and vision plans. The thresholds are adjusted upwards for certain high-risk professions, for early retirees (ages 55 to 64), for age, and for gender. The thresholds are also subject to change in the future for cost-of-living adjustments and inflation.

Hospital Insurance Tax on High–Income Individuals. Effective 2013, PPACA § 9015 increases the FICA Hospital Insurance tax by 0.9% on the wages of employees above a certain threshold. The Medicare tax will now be 2.35% on an individual's wages in excess of $200,000, or in the case of joint returns, a couple's wages in excess of $250,000. The new law also imposes a 3.8% Medicare tax on the net investment income of high-income individuals and couples, or on the excess of the wages of employees above the same threshold above, whichever is greater. Therefore, this additional Medicare tax of 3.8% will be imposed on net investment income of individuals earning $200,000 or on couples having a combined income of $250,000; or, on the excess of those amounts if it would yield a greater tax amount.

Industry Fees. The PPACA imposes significant fees on a number of health industries over time. PPACA § 9008 imposes annual fees on the pharmaceutical industry, including manufacturers and importers of branded prescription drugs, totaling approximately $28 billion starting in 2011 through 2019 and beyond. PPACA § 9010 imposes annual fees on the health insurance industry totaling approximately $59 billion starting in 2014 through 2018 and beyond. Effective 2013, PPACA § 9009 imposes a 2.3% excise tax on the price of medical devices sold by manufacturers, producers, or importers in the U.S.

TIMELINE

The provisions of the laws will be phased in between 2010 and 2018. The following implementation timeline includes some selected provisions affecting employers and employees.

<u>2010</u>

- *Small Business Tax Credit.* A tax credit of up to 35% of premiums will be available to employers with 10 or fewer employees and up to $25,000 average annual salaries and employers with 25 or fewer employees and average annual salaries up to $50,000. When exchanges are operational in 2014, tax credits will increase to 50% of premiums.

- *Eliminating Lifetime Limits.* Effective six months after enactment, lifetime limits on benefits are prohibited.

- *Regulating Use of Lifetime and Annual Limits.* Effective six months after enactment and pursuant to regulations to be issued by the Secretary of HHS, all employer-sponsored plans will be prohibited in their use of lifetime limits and restricted in their use of annual limits. When exchanges are operational in 2014, the use of annual limits will be prohibited completely.

- *Coverage of Dependents.* Effective six months after enactment, group health plans providing dependent coverage for children must make coverage available until the child becomes 26 years of age. In addition, individual and group health plans are prohibited from excluding children on the basis of a preexisting condition.

- *Early Retirees.* Effective 90 days after enactment, a new temporary reinsurance program is established to help companies that provide early retirement health benefits for individuals ages 55–64 to offset the expensive costs of the coverage.

- *Preexisting Conditions.* Individual and group health plans are prohibited from excluding children up to age 18 on the basis of a preexisting condition. Exclusion on the basis of preexisting conditions will be extended to adults in 2014. Effective 90 days after enactment until 2014, HHS will establish a temporary insurance program for uninsured people denied coverage due to pre-existing conditions.

- *Rescission.* Effective six months after enactment, individual and group health plans are prohibited from rescinding coverage, except in cases of fraud or intentional misrepresentation of material fact.

2011

- *Long–Term Care Insurance.* Effective January 1, 2011, a new long-term care insurance program will be established, financed by payroll deductions, to provide benefits to adults who become disabled.

- *Disclosure of Health Benefits.* Effective January 1, 2011, employers will be required to disclose on Form W–2 the value of the benefit provided for health insurance coverage.

2013

- *Flexible Savings Accounts.* The amount of employee contributions to flexible health savings accounts will be reduced to $2,500, indexed to the consumer price index in future years.

- *Medicare Part D Deduction.* The deduction for employers that provide prescription drug coverage to retirees under the Medicare Part D program will be eliminated.

- *Over-the-Counter Medicines.* Employees can no longer claim reimbursement for over-the-counter medicines.

2014

- *Employer Mandate.* Employers with 50 or more employees that do not offer health benefits to their full-time employees will be subject to a $2000 per employee tax penalty.

- *Automatic Enrollment.* Employers with 200 or more employees must automatically enroll all new employees in a health benefits plan.

- *Individual Mandate.* Individuals will be required to purchase health coverage or pay a tax penalty. Enrollment in an employer-sponsored plan satisfies the individual mandate. Certain exemptions are permitted.

- *Health Exchanges.* Health exchanges are established to provide access to health insurance at competitive rates; individuals with incomes up to 400% of the poverty level will be eligible for subsidies, as well as eligible small employers.

- *Free Choice Vouchers.* Employers offering minimum essential coverage through an eligible employer-sponsored plan and pay a portion of the costs will be required to offer employees a "free choice voucher" equal to the employer's cost for the plan to purchase coverage through the state exchange in lieu of enrolling in the employer's plan.

- *Waiting Periods.* Individual and group health plans may not impose waiting periods exceeding 90 days.

2018

- *High Cost Plan Excise Tax.* An excise tax of 40% will be imposed on the amount of the premium costs in excess of $10,200 for individuals and $27,500 for families.

EMPLOYER-SPONSORED EMPLOYEE HEALTH PROMOTION PLANS

Mark A. Rothstein & Heather L. Harrell, Health Risk Reduction Programs in Employer–Sponsored Health Plans: Part I–Efficacy

51 J. Occupational & Environmental Med. 943 (2009).

* * *

Health Risk Reduction Programs

The escalating costs of employee health benefits have sparked an interest by employers in reducing health care payments, especially if employee health is improved at the same time. To satisfy this growing demand, vendor companies have begun selling individualized worksite health promotion plans. According to the websites of these companies, they are now responsible for managing, to varying degrees, the health of millions of employees.

Employer-sponsored wellness and health promotion programs have been in place at numerous companies for many years. * * * Employers have recognized that many employees view health promotion programs (e.g., exercise facilities) as a benefit. They also recognize that a healthy workforce is more productive and less costly in a variety of ways (e.g., reduced sick leave, absenteeism, turnover).

The new types of health promotion programs * * * are characterized by three elements: 1) the use of HRAs [health risk assessments] to determine workers' levels of health risk; 2) the development of individualized interventions, which sometimes involves employees being frequently contacted by health advisers or "coaches" to monitor progress in risk reduction activities; and 3) the use of financial incentives, often in the form of reduced employee contributions to health benefit plans, to encourage employee participation.

Health Risk Assessments

HRAs are questionnaires completed by employees about their health practices, history, and status. The assessments are usually meant to provide a general understanding of that individual's modifiable risk factors. By contrast, biometric measurements, such as height, weight, blood pressure, and cholesterol, attempt to give numerical values to health status. Although HRAs are self-reported, biometric measures may be either self-reported or measured by intervention staff.

* * *

[I]t is difficult to develop composite models for evaluation of the accuracy or predictive ability of HRAs. Nevertheless, there is substantial evidence that HRAs can be valuable in identifying those in need of intervention to prevent disease development or progression. It is not clear, however, whether employment-based risk assessment and intervention through consulting companies are as desirable as traditional health promotion overseen by the individuals' primary care physicians.

Employee–Specific Interventions

After defining employee health risk, the next step is to devise an individual program for risk reduction. Employees may be contacted by telephone by a health adviser or coach to devise the plan. These advisers have a variety of training and expertise which may or may not be sufficient to develop an appropriate intervention for individuals with a wide range of histories, current symptoms, and medications. Other personalized approaches, such as individual feedback on the HRA, nurse help lines, or behavioral counseling, may be used independently or in combination with health coaches.

Financial Incentives

To increase participation in these voluntary programs, employers frequently offer financial inducements, such as a reduction in the employee's monthly contribution for health coverage. It is at this point that the HRRP [health risk reduction plan] stratifies workers on the basis of income. A $20 or $30 per month reduction in monthly employee contributions is not a sufficient incentive for many higher paid employees to participate. Higher paid employees are able to forego this benefit, or put another way, they can more easily afford to pay a "privacy tax" and not have to share health information with the HRRP vendor and not be bothered at home by individualized interventions. Lower paid employees may be more economically vulnerable, and thus, more likely to feel coerced into signing up to participate in the HRRP.

* * *

Conclusion

HRAs are associated with some markers of better health and lower health care costs, although this might be the result of self-selection bias. Most research indicates that individualized approaches are more effective than generalized approaches, but the data on financial incentives are more complex. Financial incentives may increase participation rates; however, the long-term effects of financial incentives on health outcomes are not as definitive and may even be negative when compared with other interventions. The magnitude of health effects of HRRPs varies considerably; the effects of these programs may last a year or longer, but the magnitude of the effect may diminish over time.

* * *

Both the methodological weaknesses [of studies evaluating the effects of HRRPs] and results of the studies lead us to question whether employers' expectations and vendors' assurances about ROI [return on investment] are realistic and accurate. Because several of the studies indicate both positive and negative health effects from HRRPs, it is reasonable to question whether the interventions could be doing more harm than good when implemented on a large scale and over the long term. Individuals responsible for deciding whether to initiate or continue HRRPs should consider whether there are alternative means to achieve the same health objectives–both at the worksite and in the clinical setting. More generally, policy makers should assess what, if any, role employers should play in the health care system and whether health promotion would be better addressed by primary care physicians than employer-sponsored health plans.

NOTES AND QUESTIONS

1. HIPAA makes it unlawful for an employer-sponsored health plan to vary premium contributions based on the health status of an employee or covered dependent, 42 U.S.C. § 300gg–1(b)(1). This provision, however, is not to be construed "to prevent a group health plan, and a health insurance issuer offering group health insurance coverage, from establishing premium discounts or rebates or modifying otherwise applicable copayments or deductibles in return for adherence to programs of health promotion and disease prevention." 42 U.S.C. § 300gg–1(b)(2).

This provision of HIPAA is jointly enforced by the Department of the Treasury, Department of Labor, and Department of Health and Human Services, which have promulgated joint rules implementing the provision. 26 C.F.R. Part 54 (Treasury), 29 C.F.R. Part 2590 (Labor), and 45 C.F.R. Part 146 (Health and Human Services). Significantly, the regulations originally limited the amount of the reward to 20% of the cost of the health plan. Section 1201 of the Patient Protection and Affordable Care Act of 2010, P.L. 111–148, increased the permissible amount of rewards to 30% of the cost of the health plan. The reward can increase to 50% if it is deemed appropriate and not a "subterfuge for discriminating based on a health status factor," or the reward is not punitive in nature. Thus, Congress has embraced health promotion inducements despite their uncertain benefits and significant ethical issues (e.g., privacy, autonomy). For a further discussion, see Mark A. Rothstein & Heather L. Harrell, Health Risk Reduction Programs in Employer–Sponsored Health Plans: Part II–Law and Ethics, 51 J. Occupational & Environmental Med. 951 (2009).

2. Health reform legislation is based on retaining and strengthening the role of employers in health care finance. Expanded health promotion activities by employers are inevitable, but are they desirable?

Page 500. Please add the following to note 3.

The Paul Wellstone and Pete Domenici Mental Health Parity and Addiction Equity Act of 2008, part of the Emergency Economic Stabilization Act of 2008, P.L. No. 110–343, prohibits group health plans with 50 or more employees from imposing any caps or limitations on mental health or substance abuse disorder benefits that are not applied to medical or surgical benefits. The Act, however, does not require plans to offer mental health or substance abuse coverage. The provisions took effect on January 1, 2010. According to government estimates, the new requirement will increase employer costs by an average of 0.4%.

Page 507. Please add the following to note 6.

"Cases awarding money damages ... exist in profusion in trust remedy law. Accordingly, money damages were and are as much an equitable remedy as a legal remedy. Justice Scalia was correct to say that 'money damages are ... the classic form of legal relief,' but flatly wrong to assert that money damages are not equally characteristic of equity when it enforces equity-based causes of action such as those arising from breach of trust." John H. Langbein, What ERISA Means by "Equitable": The Supreme Court's Trail of Error in *Russell, Mertens*, and *Great–West*, 103 Colum. L. Rev. 1317, 1337 (2003).

Page 507. Please add the following note.

7. Does section 502(a)(3) of ERISA authorize recovery of damages in the form of payment of a life insurance benefit that would have accrued but for a breach of duty by the fiduciary? Amschwand was on sick leave when Sopherion Corp. changed life insurance companies to Aetna. A Spherion executive told Amschwand he could keep his benefit even if he did not return to work for one day as the policy provided. But Spherion never put Amschwand's name on the list given to Aetna of individuals for whom the one-day-of-work requirement was being waived. Amschwand paid the premium until his death. His widow sued for the life insurance benefit. (The company did return the premium payments that had been made by Amschwand.) The court of appeals applied *Great–West*, said this would be "legal" relief, and denied the widow's claim. Amschwand v. Spherion Corp., 505 F.3d 342 (5th Cir. 2007). The U.S. Solicitor General asked the Supreme Court to grant certiorari, saying the Fifth Circuit's decision was too narrow, that there is a circuit split, and that Congress did not intend this result when it enacted ERISA. Nonetheless, certiorari was denied, ___ U.S. ___, 128 S.Ct. 2995 (2008).

C. ERISA–PREEMPTION OF STATE ACTION

Page 544. Please add the following before part D.

San Francisco enacted an ordinance, effective January 1, 2008, requiring private employers with 20 or more employees to make health care expenditures of specific amounts per hour of work. The expenditure can be in the form of contributions to a health savings account, direct reimbursement to employees, payments to third parties providing health services, and in other specified ways. A district court enjoined the ordinance on the ground that it was preempted by ERISA, but the Ninth Circuit reversed on the ground that the mandatory payments by the employer did not amount to a "plan" subject to ERISA, nor did the ordinance "relate to" an employee benefit plan. Golden Gate Restaurant Ass'n v. San Francisco, 546 F.3d 639 (9th Cir. 2008).

D. FAMILY AND MEDICAL LEAVE

Page 553. Please add the following note.

3A. The Secretary of Labor's FMLA regulations, 29 C.F.R. Part 825, were overhauled and reissued at the end of 2008. Among the numerous changes are the following: (1) if an employee submits insufficient medical documentation of the need for leave, specifically-designated parties (health care provider, human resources professional, leave administrator, or management official other than the employee's supervisor) may call the employee's health care provider for the purpose of clarifying and authenticating the employee's leave request; (2) whereas the prior version of the regulation provided that an employee had two business days after an absence to notify his or her employer of the need for FMLA leave, the new version requires the employee to use the employer's customary call-in procedures unless there are abnormal circumstances; and (3) the time spent by an employee performing light duty work does not count against the employee's FMLA leave entitlement.

Pages 554–555. Please add the following notes.

6A. Under the FMLA, an employee is required to provide the employer with notice of a request for leave. It is not necessary that the employee mention the FMLA in the request, but merely stating that he or she is sick is insufficient. In Burnett v. LFW, Inc., 472 F.3d 471 (7th Cir. 2006), the employee stated that he was sick and "wanted to go home." The Seventh Circuit held that this was adequate notice because the employer had been made aware over a four-month period that the employee was being treated for possible prostate cancer.

10. A provision of the Defense Authorization Act of 2008 amends the FMLA to permit a "spouse, son, daughter, parent, or next of kin" to take up to 26 weeks of leave to care for a member of the Armed Forces, including a member of the National Guard or Reserves, who is undergoing medical treatment, recuperation, or therapy, is otherwise in outpatient status, or is otherwise on the temporary disability retired list, for a serious injury or illness.

E. NONDISCRIMINATION IN BENEFITS

1. PREGNANCY

Page 560. Please replace the *Erickson* case with the following.

In re Union Pac. R.R. Employment Practices Litigation
479 F.3d 936 (8th Cir. 2007).

■ GRUENDER, CIRCUIT JUDGE.

Brandi Standridge and Kenya Phillips, as class representatives, sued Union Pacific Railroad Company ("Union Pacific") for sexual discrimination under Title VII of the Civil Rights Act of 1964 ("Title VII") as amended by the Pregnancy Discrimination Act of 1978 ("PDA"). The district court granted Standridge and Phillips's motion for partial summary judgment on July 15, 2005, and entered final judgment in their favor on February 10, 2006. Union Pacific appeals. For the reasons discussed below, we reverse.

I. BACKGROUND

Union Pacific, a freight company headquartered in Omaha, Nebraska, provides health care benefits to those of its employees who are covered by collective bargaining agreements ("agreement employees"). These agreement employees receive benefits through one of five plans. While the plans provide benefits for services such as routine physical exams, tetanus shots and drug and alcohol treatments, they exclude coverage of allergy serum, immunization agents, biological sera and drugs that treat infertility. They also exclude both male and female contraceptive methods, prescription and non-prescription, when used for the sole purpose of contraception. Union Pacific only covers contraception when medically necessary for a non-contraceptive purpose such as regulating menstrual cycles, treating skin problems or avoiding serious health risks associated with pregnancy.

* * *

A. PDA Analysis

As an initial matter, the district court incorrectly characterized Union Pacific's policy as the denial of prescription contraception coverage for women. Union Pacific excludes all types of contraception, whether prescription, non-prescription or surgical and whether for men or women, unless an employee has a non-contraception medical necessity for the contraception. While prescription contraception is currently only available for women, non-prescription contraception is available for men and women. Therefore, the issue is whether Union Pacific's policy of denying coverage for all contraception violates Title VII, as amended by the PDA.

Union Pacific argues that the district court erred in holding that the PDA requires coverage of contraception. It contends that the PDA only relates to discrimination against a woman for medical conditions that occur (or may occur) after she becomes pregnant, while the use of contraception only relates to human fertility before pregnancy. Standridge and Phillips argue that contraception is covered by the PDA because it is "related to" the condition of pregnancy.

Title VII provides that "[i]t shall be an unlawful employment practice for an employer ... to discriminate against any individual with respect to his compensation, terms, conditions, or privileges of employment, because of such individual's ... sex." Congress created the PDA to amend this provision in response to the Supreme Court's holding that the exclusion of pregnancy benefits did not violate Title VII. See Gen. Elec. Co. v. Gilbert, 429 U.S. 125, 145–46 (1976).

* * *

Neither the circuit courts nor the Supreme Court has considered whether the PDA applies to contraception. The Supreme Court, though, has discussed the scope of the PDA in Newport News Shipbuilding & Dry Dock Co. v. EEOC, 462 U.S. 669 (1983), and International Union, United Automobile, Aerospace & Agricultural Implement Workers of America, UAW v. Johnson Controls, Inc., 499 U.S. 187 (1991). In Newport News, the Supreme Court held that a company's health insurance plan that provided greater pregnancy benefits to its female employees than to the female spouses of its male employees was a violation of Title VII, as amended by the PDA. * * * The Court further analyzed the PDA in *Johnson Controls* in the context of a bona fide occupational qualification defense. Johnson Controls would not allow a woman who had the potential to become pregnant to work in jobs with actual or potential lead exposure because of the associated fetal health risks. The Court held that an employer could not prevent a woman from working in those positions when it did not also prevent men from working in those positions, "unless her reproductive potential prevent[ed] her from performing the duties of her job." Since reproductive potential did not prevent women from performing the duties of the positions in question, the Court held that discriminating against women on the basis of potential pregnancy was a violation of Title VII, as amended by the PDA.

In Krauel v. Iowa Methodist Medical Center, 95 F.3d 674, 679 (8th Cir. 1996), we applied these Supreme Court precedents and held that the PDA does not extend to infertility treatments. We concluded that the phrase "related medical conditions" in the PDA refers only to medical conditions associated with "pregnancy" and "childbirth," the specific terms that precede the general phrase. Infertility is "strikingly different" from pregnancy and childbirth because infertility prevents conception, while pregnancy, childbirth and medical conditions related to them can occur only after conception. Therefore, *Krauel* holds that infertility is "outside of the PDA's protection because it is not pregnancy, childbirth, or a related medical condition."

In concluding that the PDA does not extend to infertility, we also distinguished the Supreme Court's holding in *Johnson Controls*. While noting that the PDA does cover differential treatment of an employee based on health concerns that may arise during her pregnancy, we held that *Johnson Controls* does not support an expansion of the PDA to cover fertility matters prior to conception because "[p]otential pregnancy, unlike infertility, is a medical condition that is sex-related because only women can become pregnant. . . . [B]ecause the policy of denying insurance benefits for treatment of fertility problems applies to both female and male workers . . . [it] is gender-neutral. . . ."

With the guidance of these decisions, we now determine whether contraception is "related to" pregnancy for PDA purposes. While contraception may certainly affect the causal chain that leads to pregnancy, we have specifically rejected the argument that a causal connection, by itself, results in a medical condition being "related to" pregnancy for PDA purposes. Union Pacific argues that contraception, analogous to infertility, is gender-neutral. Standridge and Phillips argue that the district court correctly found that contraception implicates potential pregnancy and that the PDA covers contraception because it prevents a gender-specific condition.

Following *Krauel*, we hold that contraception is not "related to" pregnancy for PDA purposes because, like infertility treatments, contraception is a treatment that is only indicated prior to pregnancy. Contraception is not a medical treatment that occurs when or if a woman becomes pregnant; instead, contraception prevents pregnancy from even occurring. As in *Krauel*, the result in *Johnson Controls* does not require coverage of contraception because contraception is not a gender-specific term like "potential pregnancy," but rather applies to both men and women like "infertility." In conclusion, the PDA does not require coverage of contraception because contraception is not "related to" pregnancy for PDA purposes and is gender-neutral.

We are not persuaded by the contention of Standridge and Phillips and the amici members of Congress that Congress intended to address the coverage of prescription contraception in the PDA. In their views, the PDA was a "broad response" to the *Gilbert* decision, and Congress wanted to protect women in all areas concerning pregnancy, including the prevention of it. However, the plain language of the PDA makes no reference to contraception. Additionally, the House and Senate legislative histories do not mention contraception. This silence by Congress on the issue of contraception cannot be interpreted to expand the PDA to cover contraception.

We also do not agree with Standridge and Phillips's argument that the PDA's express exclusion of coverage of abortion, without an accompanying express exclusion of coverage for contraception, implies an intent to include coverage of contraception. Abortion is "the termination of a pregnancy," while contraception prevents pregnancy from even occurring. While we do not need to decide whether the PDA would cover abortion without this exclusion, abortion arguably would be "related to" pregnancy in a manner that contraception is not because abortion can only occur when a woman is pregnant. In contrast, there would be no reason for Congress to expressly exclude a treatment that is not "related to" pregnancy for PDA purposes, such as contraception.

Finally, we are not persuaded by the EEOC decision that interpreted the PDA as requiring employers to cover prescription contraception for women if they cover "other prescription drugs and devices, or other types of services, that are used to prevent the occurrences of other medical conditions." An agency's interpretation that is found in an opinion letter, policy statement, agency manual or enforcement guideline "lack[s] the force of law" and is not entitled to deference under Chevron U.S.A., Inc. v. Natural Resources Defense Council, Inc., 467 U.S. 837 (1984). This EEOC decision is similar to a policy statement or enforcement guideline, and we respect such interpretations "only to the extent that those interpretations have the 'power to persuade.' " Since Congress did not give the EEOC rule-making authority, the amount of deference we give to this decision "will depend upon the thoroughness evident in its consideration, the validity of its reasoning, its consistency with earlier and later pronouncements, and all those factors which give it power to persuade, if lacking power to control."

We find the EEOC decision to be unpersuasive. The decision addressed a policy that denied coverage of prescription contraception but included coverage of the surgical contraceptive methods of vasectomies and tubal ligations. Union Pacific's coverage is different because it excludes coverage of all contraception for women and men, both prescription and surgical. Additionally, the decision compares prescription contraception to the broadest possible spectrum of other preventive treatments and services without citing a persuasive basis for doing so. Furthermore, the EEOC did not issue any guidance on the issue of coverage of prescription contraception until 22 years after the enactment of the PDA. The delay brings into question the consistency and persuasiveness of the EEOC's position. Therefore, we find this decision unpersuasive on the question before us.

In conclusion, based on the language of the PDA and our previous holding in *Krauel*, we hold that the PDA does not encompass contraception. Contraception, like infertility treatments, is a treatment that is only indicated prior to pregnancy because contraception actually prevents pregnancy from occurring. Furthermore, like infertility, contraception is a gender-neutral term. Therefore, Union Pacific's denial of coverage for contraception for both sexes did not discriminate against its female agreement employees in violation of Title VII, as amended by the PDA.

B.   Title VII Analysis

* * *

Standridge and Phillips brought a claim of disparate treatment based on gender discrimination. To establish this disparate treatment claim, Standridge and Phillips must show, in part, that "other employees outside of the protected group were allegedly treated more favorably and were similarly situated in all relevant respects." While an employer must treat its employees similarly, it does not have to treat employees in a protected class more favorably than other employees.

In determining whether Union Pacific treated the similarly situated male employees more favorably than the protected female employees, we must compare the health benefits that Union Pacific's plans provided for men and women. The district court compared the "medicines or medical services [that] prevent employees from developing diseases or conditions that pose an equal or lesser threat to employees' health than does pregnancy." It found that the health plans treated men more favorably because the plans covered preventive medicines and services such as medication for male-pattern baldness, routine physical exams, tetanus shots, and drug and alcohol treatments. Union Pacific argues that the district court's comparator was too broad because it treated pregnancy as a disease that needed to be prevented instead of focusing on the narrow issue of contraception.

We decline to address whether pregnancy is a "disease." Instead, we simply hold that the district court erred in using the comparator "medicines or medical services [that] prevent employees from developing diseases or conditions that pose an equal or lesser threat to employees' health than does pregnancy." As previously discussed, this case concerns Union Pacific's coverage of contraception for men and women. The proper comparator is the provision of the medical benefit in question, contraception. Union Pacific's health plans do not cover any contraception used by women such as birth control, sponges, diaphragms, intrauterine devices or tubal ligations or any contraception used by men such as condoms and vasectomies. Therefore, the coverage provided to women is not less favorable than that provided to men. Thus, there is no violation of Title VII.

III. CONCLUSION

Accordingly, we reverse the district court's judgment and remand the case for further proceedings consistent with this opinion.

■ BYE, CIRCUIT JUDGE, dissenting.

* * *

The Court begins its analysis by finding the district court erred in confining its inquiry to Union Pacific's exclusion of coverage for prescription contraception used by women because its policy also excludes coverage for non-prescription contraception coverage (condoms) and surgical procedures to prevent male fertility (vasectomies). The district court did not err in limiting its inquiry to prescription contraception. That its policy does not provide coverage for condoms is unsurprising—Union Pacific has not identified any health insurance policy which would provide coverage for non-prescription, contraceptive devices available in drug stores and gas stations nationwide. As for vasectomies, even if we were to look at its exclusion of coverage for vasectomies, the policy nonetheless discriminates against females. When a policy excludes coverage for vasectomies, the medical effect of this exclusion is born entirely by women, as the record demonstrates women are the only gender which can become pregnant.

* * *

While the plain language of the PDA does not specifically include prepregnancy conditions, there is some indication Congress intended the act to cover prepregnancy discrimination. Congress used the phrase "related medical conditions." "The word 'related' indicates the PDA covers more than mere pregnancy." In this case, the district court relied on the second clause of the PDA which is drafted even more broadly than the first, covering "women *affected by* pregnancy, childbirth, or related medical conditions." Finally, as noted by certain members of Congress, writing as amici on behalf of Standridge and Phillips, the first clause of the PDA specifically states: "The terms 'because of sex' or 'on the basis of sex' *include, but are not limited to*, because of or on the basis of pregnancy, childbirth, or related medical conditions." The use of the phrase "include, but are not limited to" mandates a broad reading of the PDA because it suggests Congress was being illustrative rather than exclusive with the list following the phrase. The PDA's legislative history also promotes a broad construction of the act to include prepregnancy. Representative Ronald Sarasin explained the PDA gives a woman "the right ... to be financially and legally protected *before*, during, and after her pregnancy."

Even if Congress did not intend the PDA to cover pre-pregnancy discrimination, the Supreme Court ostensibly broadened the scope of the PDA to include pre-pregnancy discrimination in International Union, United Automobile, Aerospace & Agricultural Implement Workers, UAW v. Johnson Controls, Inc., 499 U.S. 187 (1991). The Court found classifying employees on the basis of childbearing capacity, whether or not they were already pregnant, "must be regarded, for Title VII purposes, in the same light as explicit sex discrimination." In *Johnson Controls*, a battery manufacturer enforced a gender-based, fetal-protection policy excluding fertile women (women who were pregnant or capable of becoming pregnant) from working in jobs where they would be exposed to lead. The bias was clear, as the policy at issue excluded only women. The Court used the PDA to bolster its holding the policy discriminated on its face as it "explicitly classifies on the basis of potential for pregnancy." The choice to treat all "female employees as potentially pregnant" was discriminatory.

* * *

Potential pregnancy, like infertility, by its definition occurs prior to conception. The same can be said for the use of prescription contraception. The reason *Krauel* determined the PDA did not apply to an employer's failure to cover infertility treatments, even in light of *Johnson Controls*, was because infertility, unlike potential pregnancy, is a gender-neutral affliction. After *Krauel*, denial of coverage for infertility treatments does not implicate the PDA because infertility affects both men and women. The Court suggests infertility treatments and contraception are both prepregnancy and this fact makes the difference. Although both are used prior to conception, when one looks at the medical effect of the denial of insurance coverage, prescription contraception is easily distinguishable from infertility treatments. As the district court aptly notes: "Health plans that deny coverage for *contraception*, by definition, affect only the health of *women*." With prescription contraception a woman controls her potential pregnancy. Such contraception is necessarily gender-related because it prevents pregnancy only in women. Without contraception, a sexually active, fertile woman is almost certain to become pregnant Once pregnant, only the woman's health is affected. Infertility, by contrast, is a word used to describe a number of medical conditions affecting both men and women. When a man or a woman is infertile, he or she is unable to contribute to reproduction as his or her reproductive organs do not function properly. Infertility treatments may correct the medical condition of infertility in both men and women, allowing them to effectively make the necessary contribution to reproduction. Thus, prescription contraception and infertility treatments are like apples and oranges. Although both relate to pregnancy in a general sense, prescription contraception is, unlike fertility treatments, at its very core gender-specific. As such, a PDA claim based on a failure to provide prescription contraception coverage is not foreclosed by *Krauel*. More importantly, the Court's holding here—"that contraception is not 'related to' pregnancy for PDA purposes because, like infertility treatments, contraception is a treatment that is only indicated prior to pregnancy," is inconsistent with *Johnson Controls*.

In addition to holding the PDA does not apply under *Krauel*, the Court also holds Union Pacific's policy does not discriminate against women under Title VII, because the policy excludes contraception coverage for both men and women. Because I agree with the district court's comparison— between the insurance coverage provided to men and woman for all types of preventative medicine—I also dissent with regard to this holding.

NOTES AND QUESTIONS

1.   *Union Pacific* is the first circuit court decision on the issue. The district court decisions are split on whether the PDA requires companies to provide coverage for contraception.

2.   The majority relies on the timing of contraception to equate it with infertility treatment as not being covered under the PDA. The dissent relies on the effects of the lack of contraception to assert that contraception is "related" to pregnancy. Both opinions rely on the legislative history in attempting to buttress their arguments.

3.   Do you agree with the dissent that failure to cover vasectomies would constitute sex discrimination against women because only women get pregnant?

4.   For a further discussion, see Stephen F. Befort & Elizabeth C. Borer, Equitable Prescription Drug Coverage in Employer–Provided Health Plans, 70 La. L. Rev. 205 (2009).

3.   SEXUAL ORIENTATION

Page 576.   Please add the following after note 2.

2A.   New Jersey has since reversed course. In Lewis v. Harris, 908 A.2d 196 (N.J. 2006), the New Jersey Supreme Court held that same-sex couples must be afforded the same rights and benefits as those enjoyed by married heterosexual couples. "Although we cannot find that a fundamental right to same-sex marriage exists in this State, the unequal dispensation of rights and benefits to committed same-sex partners can no longer be tolerated under our Constitution."

Page 577.   Please add the following notes.

8.   Patricia Martinez and her same-sex partner, Lisa Ann Golden, were married in Canada. Martinez' subsequent application for spousal health care benefits from her New York employer was denied because of the employer's policy of only providing health care benefits for the opposite-sex spouses of its employees. The court held that, absent express legislation to the contrary, New York recognizes lawful marriages in other jurisdictions. Therefore, the employer discriminated on the basis of sexual orientation in violation of New York law. Martinez v. County of Monroe, 850 N.Y.S.2d 740 (App. Div. 2008).

9.   On June 17, 2009, President Obama signed a Presidential Memorandum, 74 Fed. Reg. 29,393 (2009), extending some benefits to the same-sex partners of federal employees, including the ability to take leave to care for sick partners and making long-term care insurance available to same-sex partners. The Defense of Marriage Act bars the federal government from extending health care coverage to the same-sex partners of federal employees. The proposed Domestic Partners Benefits and Obligations Act would extend such benefits to same-sex couples.

CHAPTER 7

FREEDOM IN THE WORKPLACE

A. GROOMING AND DRESS

Page 584. Please add the following to note 5.

Cf. Webb v. City of Philadelphia, 562 F.3d 256 (3d Cir. 2009) (no Title VII violation where police department could not accommodate an officer's request to wear a Muslim headscarf without undue hardship).

Page 592. Please add the following note.

4A. For a further discussion, see Dianne Avery & Marion Crain, Branded: Corporate Image, Sexual Stereotyping, and the New Face of Capitalism, 14 Duke J. Gender L. & Pol'y 13 (2007).

Page 593. Please add the following note.

7. A Muslim woman who wore a khimar or long headscarf applied to a temporary employment agency and was considered for referral to a job working for a printing company. When she said she could not remove her headscarf, the temp agency refused to refer her because the company had a dress policy prohibiting all headwear and loose-fitting clothing. Has the temp agency engaged in discrimination based on religion? See EEOC v. Kelly Services, Inc., 598 F.3d 1022 (8th Cir. 2010) (held: no violation of Title VII because employer, whose employees worked with printing presses and similar machinery, had legitimate safety justification for its rule, and there was no evidence that the rule was pretextual).

A similar case involved the Philadelphia Police Department, which disciplined an officer for wearing a Muslim hijab, a headscarf that sometimes includes a veil, to work on two occasions, thereby violating a department rule prohibiting the wearing of religious attire while on duty.

The Third Circuit rejected the religious discrimination claim, holding that the department had an overriding interest in maintaining the uniform appearance of its officers. Webb v. Philadelphia, 562 F.3d 256 (3d Cir. 2009).

Page 602. Please add the following to note 2.

Bills to prohibit workplace bullying have been introduced into at least a dozen state legislatures, but none has yet been enacted.

Page 604. Please add the following to note 6.

See also Yuknis v. First Student, Inc., 481 F.3d 552 (7th Cir. 2007).

Page 615. Please add the following to note 1.

See also Clair Diefenbach, Same–Sex Harassment After *Oncale*: Meeting the "Because of . . . Sex" Requirement, 22 Berkeley J. Gender, L. & Justice 42 (2007).

B. HARASSMENT

Page 610. Please insert the following notes.

4A. To be actionable under Title VII, the adverse treatment must be because of an individual's sex or other characteristic subject to the statute. For example, in Brown v. Henderson, 257 F.3d 246 (2d Cir. 2001), the plaintiff was subject to harassment, but the overwhelming evidence indicated that the basis of the harassment was a dispute over a union election, "and not from being a woman."

5A. Employers have a duty to prevent harassment by third parties that has the effect of creating a hostile workplace environment. In Beckford v. Department of Corrections, 605 F.3d 951 (11th Cir. 2010), 14 female former employees at a state correctional facility sued the state based on pervasive sexual harassment perpetrated by male inmates. The Eleventh Circuit held that the defendant made almost no effort to protect the women employees and that reasonable remedial measures were available, including referring the incidents for criminal prosecution.

Page 621. Please add the following note.

3A. Section 4207 of the Patient Protection and Affordable Care Act of 2010, P.L. 111–148, amends the FLSA to require that employers provide "reasonable break time" and a "suitable place" other than a bathroom for an employee to express breast milk for her nursing child. Employers with fewer than 50 employees are exempt from the requirements if compliance would impose a hardship.

C. PRIVACY

Page 622. Please add the following note before _Vega–Rodriguez_.

7. John Doe, a hospital employee, attempted to commit suicide by taking an overdose of aspirin. Thereafter, he was hospitalized in the mental health unit. While hospitalized, there was improper access to Doe's medical and mental health records by hospital employees. Doe alleged that the disclosures caused him additional emotional distress. In affirming the grant of post-trial judgment to the hospital, the Iowa Supreme Court held that Doe failed to prove a causal link between the unauthorized access to his health records and further emotional distress. "We conclude that lay jurors, unaided by expert testimony, could not distinguish the emotional distress, if any, arising from the unauthorized disclosures of Doe's records from the preexisting emotional distress." Doe v. Central Iowa Health Sys., 766 N.W.2d 787 (Iowa 2009). Does the HIPAA Privacy Rule, p. 500 note 2, afford Doe any relief? There is no private right of action under HIPAA.

Page 628. Please delete _Fraser_ and replace with the following:

City of Ontario v. Quon
130 S.Ct. 2619 (2010).

■ JUSTICE KENNEDY delivered the opinion of the Court.

This case involves the assertion by a government employer of the right, in circumstances to be described, to read text messages sent and received on a pager the employer owned and issued to an employee. The employee contends that the privacy of the messages is protected by the ban on "unreasonable searches and seizures" found in the Fourth Amendment to the United States Constitution, made applicable to the States by the Due Process Clause of the Fourteenth Amendment. Though the case touches issues of far reaching significance, the Court concludes it can be resolved by settled principles determining when a search is reasonable.

The City of Ontario (City) is a political subdivision of the State of California. The case arose out of incidents in 2001 and 2002 when respondent Jeff Quon was employed by the Ontario Police Department (OPD). He was a police sergeant and member of OPD's Special Weapons and Tactics (SWAT) Team.

* * *

In October 2001, the City acquired 20 alphanumeric pagers capable of sending and receiving text messages. Arch Wireless Operating Company provided wireless service for the pagers. Under the City's service contract with Arch Wireless, each pager was allotted a limited number of characters sent or received each month. Usage in excess of that amount would result in an additional fee. The City issued pagers to Quon and other SWAT Team members in order to help the SWAT Team mobilize and respond to emergency situations.

Before acquiring the pagers, the City announced a "Computer Usage, Internet and E–Mail Policy" (Computer Policy) that applied to all employees. Among other provisions, it specified that the City "reserves the right to monitor and log all network activity including e-mail and Internet use, with or without notice. Users should have no expectation of privacy or confidentiality when using these resources." In March 2000, Quon signed a statement acknowledging that he had read and understood the Computer Policy.

The Computer Policy did not apply, on its face, to text messaging. Text messages share similarities with e-mails, but the two differ in an important way. In this case, for instance, an e-mail sent on a City computer was transmitted through the City's own data servers, but a text message sent on one of the City's pagers was transmitted using wireless radio frequencies from an individual pager to a receiving station owned by Arch Wireless. It was routed through Arch Wireless' computer network, where it remained until the recipient's pager or cellular telephone was ready to receive the message, at which point Arch Wireless transmitted the message from the transmitting station nearest to the recipient. After delivery, Arch Wireless retained a copy on its computer servers. The message did not pass through computers owned by the City.

Although the Computer Policy did not cover text messages by its explicit terms, the City made clear to employees, including Quon, that the City would treat text messages the same way as it treated e-mails. At an April 18, 2002, staff meeting at which Quon was present, Lieutenant Steven Duke, the OPD officer responsible for the City's contract with Arch Wireless, told officers that messages sent on the pagers "are considered e-mail messages. This means that [text] messages would fall under the City's policy as public information and [would be] eligible for auditing." Duke's comments were put in writing in a memorandum sent on April 29, 2002, by Chief Scharf to Quon and other City personnel.

Within the first or second billing cycle after the pagers were distributed, Quon exceeded his monthly text message character allotment. Duke told Quon about the overage, and reminded him that messages sent on the pagers were "considered e-mail and could be audited." Duke said, however, that "it was not his intent to audit [an] employee's text messages to see if the overage [was] due to work related transmissions." Duke suggested that Quon could reimburse the City for the overage fee rather than have Duke audit the messages. Quon wrote a check to the City for the overage. Duke offered the same arrangement to other employees who incurred overage fees.

Over the next few months, Quon exceeded his character limit three or four times. Each time he reimbursed the City. Quon and another officer again incurred overage fees for their pager usage in August 2002. At a meeting in October, Duke told Scharf that he had become " 'tired of being a bill collector.' " Scharf decided to determine whether the existing character limit was too low—that is, whether officers such as Quon were having to pay fees for sending work-related messages—or if the overages were for personal messages. Scharf told Duke to request transcripts of text messages sent in August and September by Quon and the other employee who had exceeded the character allowance.

At Duke's request, an administrative assistant employed by OPD contacted Arch Wireless. After verifying that the City was the subscriber on the accounts, Arch Wireless provided the desired transcripts. Duke reviewed the transcripts and discovered that many of the messages sent and received on Quon's pager were not work related, and some were sexually explicit. Duke reported his findings to Scharf, who, along with Quon's immediate supervisor, reviewed the transcripts himself. After his review, Scharf referred the matter to OPD's internal affairs division for an investigation into whether Quon was violating OPD rules by pursuing personal matters while on duty.

The officer in charge of the internal affairs review was Sergeant Patrick McMahon. Before conducting a review, McMahon used Quon's work schedule to redact the transcripts in order to eliminate any messages Quon sent while off duty. He then reviewed the content of the messages Quon sent during work hours. McMahon's report noted that Quon sent or received 456 messages during work hours in the month of August 2002, of which no more than 57 were work related; he sent as many as 80 messages during a single day at work; and on an average workday, Quon sent or received 28 messages, of which only 3 were related to police business. The report concluded that Quon had violated OPD rules. Quon was allegedly disciplined.

Raising claims under Rev. Stat. § 1979, 42 U.S.C. § 1983; 18 U.S.C. § 2701 et seq., popularly known as the Stored Communications Act (SCA); and California law, Quon filed suit against petitioners in the United States District Court for the Central District of California. * * * Among the allegations in the complaint was that petitioners violated respondents' Fourth Amendment rights and the SCA by obtaining and reviewing the transcript of Jeff Quon's pager messages and that Arch Wireless had violated the SCA by turning over the transcript to the City.

* * *

The Fourth Amendment states: "The right of the people to be secure in their persons, houses, papers, and effects, against unreasonable searches and seizures, shall not be violated. . . . " It is well settled that the Fourth Amendment's protection extends beyond the sphere of criminal investigations. Camara v. Municipal Court of City and County of San Francisco, 387 U.S. 523, 530 (1967). "The Amendment guarantees the privacy, dignity, and security of persons against certain arbitrary and invasive acts by officers of the Government," without regard to whether the government actor is investigating crime or performing another function. Skinner v. Railway Labor Executives' Assn., 489 U.S. 602, 613–614 (1989). The Fourth Amendment applies as well when the Government acts in its capacity as an employer. Treasury Employees v. Von Raab, 489 U.S. 656, 665 (1989).

The Court discussed this principle in O'Connor [v. Ortega, 480 U.S. 709 (1987)]. There a physician employed by a state hospital alleged that hospital officials investigating workplace misconduct had violated his Fourth Amendment rights by searching his office and seizing personal items from his desk and filing cabinet. All Members of the Court agreed with the general principle that "[i]ndividuals do not lose Fourth Amendment rights merely because they work for the government instead of a private employer." A majority of the Court further agreed that " 'special needs, beyond the normal need for law enforcement,' " make the warrant and probable-cause requirement impracticable for government employers.

* * *

Later, in the *Von Raab* decision, the Court explained that "operational realities" could diminish an employee's privacy expectations, and that this diminution could be taken into consideration when assessing the reasonableness of a workplace search. In the two decades since *O'Connor*, however, the threshold test for determining the scope of an employee's Fourth Amendment rights has not been clarified further. Here, though they disagree on whether Quon had a reasonable expectation of privacy, both petitioners and respondents start from the premise that the *O'Connor* plurality controls. It is not necessary to resolve whether that premise is correct. The case can be decided by determining that the search was reasonable even assuming Quon had a reasonable expectation of privacy.

* * *

The Court must proceed with care when considering the whole concept of privacy expectations in communications made on electronic equipment owned by a government employer. The judiciary risks error by elaborating too fully on the Fourth Amendment implications of emerging technology before its role in society has become clear. * * * It is not so clear that courts at present are on so sure a ground. Prudence counsels caution before the facts in the instant case are used to establish far-reaching premises that define the existence, and extent, of privacy expectations enjoyed by employees when using employer-provided communication devices.

Rapid changes in the dynamics of communication and information transmission are evident not just in the technology itself but in what society accepts as proper behavior. As one *amici* brief notes, many employers expect or at least tolerate personal use of such equipment by employees because it often increases worker efficiency. Another *amicus* points out that the law is beginning to respond to these developments, as some States have recently passed statutes requiring employers to notify employees when monitoring their electronic communications. At present, it is uncertain how workplace norms, and the law's treatment of them, will evolve.

Even if the Court were certain that the *O'Connor* plurality's approach were the right one, the Court would have difficulty predicting how employees' privacy expectations will be shaped by those changes or the degree to which society will be prepared to recognize those expectations as reasonable. Cell phone and text message communications are so pervasive that some persons may consider them to be essential means or necessary instruments for self-expression, even self-identification. That might strengthen the case for an expectation of privacy. On the other hand, the ubiquity of those devices has made them generally affordable, so one could counter that employees who need cell phones or similar devices for personal matters can purchase and pay for their own. And employer policies concerning communications will of course shape the reasonable expectations of their employees, especially to the extent that such policies are clearly communicated.

A broad holding concerning employees' privacy expectations vis-à-vis employer-provided technological equipment might have implications for future cases that cannot be predicted. It is preferable to dispose of this case on narrower grounds. For present purposes we assume several propositions *arguendo*: First, Quon had a reasonable expectation of privacy in the text messages sent on the pager provided to him by the City; second, petitioners' review of the transcript constituted a search within the meaning of the Fourth Amendment; and third, the principles applicable to a government employer's search of an employee's physical office apply with at least the same force when the employer intrudes on the employee's privacy in the electronic sphere.

Even if Quon had a reasonable expectation of privacy in his text messages, petitioners did not necessarily violate the Fourth Amendment by obtaining and reviewing the transcripts. Although as a general matter, warrantless searches "are *per se* unreasonable under the Fourth Amendment," there are "a few specifically established and well-delineated exceptions" to that general rule. The Court has held that the " 'special needs' " of the workplace justify one such exception.

Under the approach of the *O'Connor* plurality, when conducted for a "noninvestigatory, work-related purpos[e]" or for the "investigatio[n] of work-related misconduct," a government employer's warrantless search is reasonable if it is " 'justified at its inception' " and if " 'the measures adopted are reasonably related to the objectives of the search and not excessively intrusive in light of' " the circumstances giving rise to the search. The search here satisfied the standard of the *O'Connor* plurality and was reasonable under that approach.

The search was justified at its inception because there were "reasonable grounds for suspecting that the search [was] necessary for a noninvestigatory work-related purpose." As a jury found, Chief Scharf ordered the search in order to determine whether the character limit on the City's contract with Arch Wireless was sufficient to meet the City's needs. This was, as the Ninth Circuit noted, a "legitimate work-related rationale." The City and OPD had a legitimate interest in ensuring that employees were not being forced to pay out of their own pockets for work-related expenses, or on the other hand that the City was not paying for extensive personal communications.

As for the scope of the search, reviewing the transcripts was reasonable because it was an efficient and expedient way to determine whether Quon's overages were the result of work-related messaging or personal use. The review was also not " 'excessively intrusive.' " Although Quon had gone over his monthly allotment a number of times, OPD requested transcripts for only the months of August and September 2002. While it may have been reasonable as well for OPD to review transcripts of all the months in which Quon exceeded his allowance, it was certainly reasonable for OPD to review messages for just two months in order to obtain a large enough sample to decide whether the character limits were efficacious. And it is worth noting that during his internal affairs investigation, McMahon redacted all messages Quon sent while off duty, a measure which reduced the intrusiveness of any further review of the transcripts.

Furthermore, and again on the assumption that Quon had a reasonable expectation of privacy in the contents of his messages, the extent of an expectation is relevant to assessing whether the search was too intrusive. Even if he could assume some level of privacy would inhere in his messages, it would not have been reasonable for Quon to conclude that his messages were in all circumstances immune from scrutiny. Quon was told that his messages were subject to auditing. As a law enforcement officer, he would or should have known that his actions were likely to come under legal scrutiny, and that this might entail an analysis of his on-the-job communications. Under the circumstances, a reasonable employee would be aware that sound management principles might require the audit of messages to determine whether the pager was being appropriately used.

* * *

Because the search was reasonable, petitioners did not violate respondents' Fourth Amendment rights, and the court below erred by concluding otherwise. The judgment of the Court of Appeals for the Ninth Circuit is reversed, and the case is remanded for further proceedings consistent with this opinion.

■ JUSTICE STEVENS, concurring.

* * *

■ JUSTICE SCALIA, concurring in part and concurring in the judgment.

* * *

NOTES AND QUESTIONS

1.   Does the ubiquity of pagers, e-mail, cell phones, and similar forms of communications technology suggest that employees have greater or lesser expectations of privacy in their communications? To what extent is your answer influenced by the public/private nature of the employment or more specific facts of a particular job?

2.   In its decision, the Ninth Circuit held that the search was unreasonable. It pointed to less intrusive methods of reviewing Quon's pager use, including reminding him that he was forbidden from using his pager for personal communications and that the contents would be subject to audit to ensure that the pager was only used for work-related purposes. It also suggested that it could have asked Quon to count the characters himself or asked him to redact personal messages and grant the OPD permission to review the redacted transcript. The Supreme Court held this was unnecessary. "Even assuming there were ways that OPD could have performed the search that would have been less intrusive, it does not follow that the search was unreasonable." Do you agree?

3.   In his opinion, Justice Kennedy was careful to avoid stating principles of electronic communication privacy in the workplace more broadly because communications technology is changing so rapidly. Was the Court too timid and too limited in its pronouncements to afford sufficient guidance or was it being wise and cautious?

4.   For a proposal to enact federal legislation in the area, see Ariana R. Levinson, Carpe Diem: Privacy Protection in Employment Act, 43 Akron L. Rev. 331 (2010).

Page 632.   Please add the following to note 2.

See Orin S. Kerr, A User's Guide to the Stored Communications Act, and a Legislator's Guide to Amending It, 72 Geo. Wash. L. Rev. 1208 (2004).

Page 632.   Please add the following to note 3.

See also Miller v. Blattner, 676 F.Supp.2d 485 (E.D. La. 2009) (employee had no reasonable expectation of privacy with regard to e-mails on his work computer because his employer had a published policy prohibiting personal use of the computers and the e-mails were directly relevant to the employee's performance).

Page 633.   Please add the following note.

7A.   Three employees were disciplined by the City of Bridgeport for improper job performance based on information obtained by the use of GPS devices on the city-owned vehicles driven by the employees. The employees were not informed about the GPS tracking, and they sued claiming that the city was precluded from disciplining them because it violated Conn. Gen. Stat. § 31–48d, which prohibits an employer from electronically monitoring an employee's activities without first providing notice to the employee. The

Connecticut Supreme Court held that the statute did not provide for an express or implied right of action in favor of the employees. The only remedy is enforcement by the state labor commissioner. Gerardi v. City of Bridgeport, 985 A.2d 328 (Conn. 2010).

8. In LVRC Holdings v. Brekka, 581 F.3d 1127 (9th Cir. 2009), an employer sued its former employee alleging the employee violated the federal Computer Fraud and Abuse Act by accessing its computer "without authorization." The employee had permission to use the computer, but he did not have permission to e-mail certain confidential documents to himself and his wife. The documents included a customer list and a financial statement. The court held that "authorization" under the statute was synonymous with "permission," and therefore a statutory action could be brought against the former employee.

9. The European Court of Human Rights held that the an employer's monitoring, without providing notice, of an employee's e-mail and telephone conversations to determine whether the employee was using the employer's facilities for personal purposes was unlawful. Article 8 of the Convention for the Protection of Human Rights and Fundamental Freedoms provides that: "Everyone has the right to respect for his private and family life, his home and his correspondence." The court held that the provision applied to workplaces as well as other settings. Copland v. United Kingdom, [2007] ECHR 253 (2007).

D. FREEDOM OF EXPRESSION

Page 651. Please add the following notes.

1A. How far should *Garcetti* extend? David Weintraub, a fifth grade public school teacher in Brooklyn, New York, was discharged after he filed a grievance over his employer's refusal to discipline a student who threw a book at him on two consecutive days. *Garcetti* held that the First Amendment does not protect speech made pursuant to an employee's official duties. The Board of Education argued that Weintraub's filing of the grievance was "speech in furtherance of official duties" and therefore not protected by the First Amendment. See Weintraub v. Board of Education, 593 F.3d 196 (2d Cir. 2010) (upholding dismissal). If, instead of filing a grievance, Weintraub had led a protest march through the streets of Brooklyn, would his actions have been protected?

2A. In Jordan v. Ector County, 516 F.3d 290 (5th Cir. 2008), Jordan, an employee in the local clerk's office, ran for the position of clerk and was defeated by Morgan, who then became her supervisor. Four years later, as the next election loomed, with Jordan not yet having announced her plans, she was fired. Jordan sued alleging retaliation for exercising her First Amendment rights. The Fifth Circuit held that Jordan engaged in activities involving a hybrid of speech and political affiliation that are protected by the First Amendment. The court determined that a reasonable jury could conclude that Jordan's first attempt at office or her continuing affiliation as Morgan's rival was a substantial and motivating reason for her discharge.

Page 651. Please add the following to note 5.

See also D'Angelo v. School Board, 497 F.3d 1203 (11th Cir. 2007) (*Garcetti* applies to freedom to petition and freedom of association cases).

F.   REGULATION OF OFF-WORK ACTIVITY

1.   PERSONAL ASSOCIATIONS

Page 662. Please add the following note.

4A. Following an extramarital affair by two employees, an employer discharged the female employee but retained the male employee. The evidence indicated that the employer knew of 12 other employees who engaged in extramarital affairs and did not discipline either employee, the employer discharged the female employee because of fear that her husband might cause a disruption at the workplace, and the male employee was a top producer. In a Title VII case alleging sex discrimination, what result? See Hossack v. Floor Covering Assocs. of Joliet, Inc., 492 F.3d 853 (7th Cir. 2007) (held: no violation; plaintiff failed to introduce sufficient evidence of intentional discrimination).

Page 668. Please add the following note.

7A. Melissa Poirier, a state corrections officer was discharged for having "contact" with a former inmate. In rejecting her claim based on freedom of association, the First Circuit held that the state's interest in preserving prison security was advanced by its policy prohibiting guards from having relationships with current or former inmates. Poirier v. Massachusetts Dep't of Correction, 558 F.3d 92 (1st Cir. 2009).

7B. Randolph Starling, a "rescue captain" with the Palm Beach County Fire Rescue Department, sued under 42 U.S.C. § 1983 alleging he was denied his First Amendment right to intimate association when he was demoted for having an extramarital affair with Carolyn Smith, one of his subordinates. The Eleventh Circuit upheld the public employer's action because its interest in discouraging intimate association between supervisors and subordinates was so critical to the effective functioning of the fire department that it outweighed Starling's interest. Starling v. Board of County Commissioners, 602 F.3d 1257 (11th Cir. 2010).

2.   POLITICAL ACTIVITY

Page 677. Please add the following notes.

6. In Greenwell v. Parsley, 541 F.3d 401 (6th Cir. 2008), the Sixth Circuit upheld the discharge of a deputy sheriff when the sheriff read in the newspaper that the deputy was planning to run against him in the next election. The court noted that the firing was not based on political beliefs or affiliations.

7.   Kathleen Nichols worked for the county school district for nine years, the last six as an administrative assistant to Jeffrey Blanck, the general counsel of the district. When Blanck "had problems" with the school superintendent, an open meeting of the board's trustees was called to determine his future. The board voted to terminate Blanck. Nichols attended the meeting and sat next to Blanck. She later answered a call from Blanck and told him that an outside counsel was coming into the office, that the head of human resources had requested a list of ongoing matters, and that Nichols was going to be taking some time off. When the head of human resources accused her of disloyalty, Nichols retired and sued under a theory of retaliation. The Ninth Circuit rejected the claim that Nichols was fired because of her political activities, holding that she was fired because of her association with Blanck, and that the patronage dismissal doctrine does not apply to claims involving personal rather than political loyalty. Nichols v. Dancer, 567 F.3d 423 (9th Cir. 2009).

CHAPTER 8

OCCUPATIONAL SAFETY AND HEALTH

A. INTRODUCTION

2. JURISDICTION

Page 711. Please add the following note.

9. In Ramsey Winch, Inc. v. Henry, 555 F.3d 1199 (10th Cir. 2009), several employers challenged an Oklahoma law requiring property owners to permit firearms on their property. The district court held that the law is preempted by the OSH Act, which generally requires employers to prevent workplace hazards. The Tenth Circuit reversed, noting that OSHA has declined to adopt any standard dealing with firearms in the workplace. But cf. Plona v. United Parcel Service, Inc., 558 F.3d 478 (6th Cir. 2009) (employer's discharge of an employee for possessing firearm in vehicle in company parking lot did not violate a clear public policy in Ohio). See generally Dayna B. Royal, Take Your Gun to Work and Leave It in the Parking Lot: Why the OSH Act Does Not Preempt State Guns-at-Work Laws, 61 Fla. L. Rev. 475 (2009).

C. EMPLOYER DUTIES

1. COMPLIANCE WITH STANDARDS

Page 741. Please add the following note.

6. In Solis v. Summit Contractors, Inc., 558 F.3d 815 (8th Cir. 2009), the Eighth Circuit reversed the Commission and upheld the Secretary's policy of citing general contractors on construction sites for violations of subcontractors, so long as the general contractor had employees at the site, even if they were not exposed to the particular hazard.

CHAPTER 9

Disabling Injury and Illness

B. Workers' Compensation Coverage

3. "Course of Employment"

Page 798. Please add the following to note 3.

See Michalak v. Liberty Northwest Ins. Corp., 175 P.3d 893 (Mont. 2008) (employee injured riding wave runner at company picnic was within the course and scope of his employment).

Page 798. Please add the following to note 4.

In Ball–Foster Glass Container Co. v. Giovanelli, 177 P.3d 692 (Wash. 2008), an employee was on a business trip for his employer. As he was walking across the street from his hotel to a music performance in the park, he was struck by a car and very seriously injured. Adopting the "traveling employee" doctrine, the Supreme Court of Washington held that the claimant's injuries were compensable because his actions did not "distinctly depart" from the course of employment on a "personal errand."

4A. Frantz Pierre, a lawfully admitted migrant farmworker from Haiti, fractured his ankle when he fell, during non-work time, on a wet sidewalk at the housing provided by the company. South Carolina's workers' compensation agency denied his claim because he was not injured while working and he was not required to live in the housing provided by the employer. The South Carolina Circuit Court affirmed, but the South Carolina Supreme Court reversed. It held that because the source of Mr. Pierre's injury was a risk associated with the conditions under which the employees lived, the injury was covered by workers' compensation. South Carolina thus joined the majority of jurisdictions to adopt the "bunkhouse rule," holding compensable employee injuries sustained at employer-provided housing. Pierre v. Seaside Farms, 689 S.E.2d 615 (S.C. 2010). Compare *Frank Diehl*, supra p. 700.

Page 798. Please add the following to note 6.

See Hilton v. Martin, 654 S.E.2d 572 (Va. 2008) (paramedic who died of electrocution and cardiac arrest after being hit with a charged defibrilator by co-employee was not injured in the course of her employment, thereby permitting her estate's negligence claims to proceed).

C. OCCUPATIONAL DISEASE

2. BURDEN OF PROOF

Page 807.   Please insert the following note.

1A. Workers' compensation mental distress cases generally fall into one of the following three categories: (1) physical-mental, where a work-related physical injury leads to mental distress; (2) mental-physical, where work-related mental distress leads to physical manifestations; and (3) mental-mental, where a work-related mental distress leads to mental illness. The third category of cases has proven to be the most difficult for claimants.

Page 807.   Please add the following to note 3.

But see Kelly v. State Department of Corrections, 218 P.3d 291 (Alaska 2009) (prison guard who suffered severe emotional distress after being threatened by convicted murderer demonstrated that his stress was "extraordinary and unusual" in comparison to co-workers as required by the statute); Family Dollar Stores, Inc. v. Edwards, 245 S.W.3d 181 (Ark. Ct. App. 2006) (cashier who suffered heart attack one day after being robbed at gunpoint entitled to compensation).

Page 807.   Please add the following to note 4.

See also Carpenter's Case, 923 N.E.2d 1026 (Mass. 2010) (widow of employee who suffered sudden cardiac death while operating snow blower was entitled to compensation, notwithstanding the employee's preexisting coronary artery disease).

5. Is an employee, a part-time practical nurse at a nursing home, entitled to workers' compensation for aggravation of her preexisting chronic obstructive pulmonary disease caused by inhaling perfume sprayed by a co-employee in the workplace? See Sexton v. County of Cumberland/Cumberland Manor, 962 A.2d 1114 (N.J.Super.A.D. 2009) (held: yes).

6. In Estate of George v. Vermont League of Cities, 993 A.2d 367 (Vt. 2010), the Supreme Court of Vermont held that the claimants failed to prove that the death of a 36–year fire department employee from non-Hodgkin's lymphoma was more probable than not caused by job-related exposures. The court upheld the trial court's application of the epidemiological odds ratio of 2.0, meaning that the risk of disease more than doubles from exposure. Thus, the trial court correctly excluded claimant's expert testimony that purported to show an association between exposure and disease, but with an odds ratio of less than 2.0.

7. In many jurisdictions the statute of limitations differs for occupational disease and occupational injury cases and therefore the categorization of a claim is sometimes very important. Yet, the difference between a disease and an injury is not always clear. In IBP, Inc. v. Burress, 779 N.W.2d 210 (Iowa 2009), an employee who slaughtered pigs at a packing plant was diagnosed with brucellosis (also called undulant fever) six years after his last exposure on the job. Brucellosis is a serious bacterial infection often caused by exposure to animal blood. The claimant's physician told him that he had contracted brucellosis from hog blood, with skin abrasions being the most common portal of entry. The Iowa Supreme Court held that brucellosis was an injury, rather than a disease, because it had its origin in a traumatic injury, a cut or an abrasion. The longer statute of limitations for injuries meant that the claim was not time-barred.

D. DETERMINING BENEFIT LEVELS

2. REHABILITATION AND OTHER SERVICES

Page 823. Please add the following to note 4.

See Simmons v. Comfort Suites, 968 A.2d 1123 (Md. 2009) (jury question whether a home security system was compensable for claimant who suffered from post-traumatic stress disorder and other serious physical and mental problems after brutal attack at work during an attempted robbery); Beelman Trucking v. Workers' Comp. Comm'n, 886 N.E.2d 479 (Ill. Ct. App. 2008) (voice-activated computer system for extensively injured claimant held to be compensable); Griffiths v. Workers' Comp. Appeal Bd., 943 A.2d 242 (Pa. 2008) (wheelchair accessible van for quadriplegic claimant held to be compensable "orthopedic appliance").

E. TORT ACTIONS AND "EXCLUSIVITY"

1. ACTIONS AGAINST THE EMPLOYER

Page 837. Please add the following note.

2A. Some courts resolve the issue without resort to the dual capacity rule by considering whether the employee's injuries "arose out of employment." In one case, the plaintiff, a pain-management physician, was experiencing ankle pain from an off-work source when her colleague offered to administer a nerve block injection. After a second injection a few days later, the plaintiff developed complications requiring surgery. The D.C. Court of Appeals held that the injections did not arise out of her employment and therefore a medical malpractice action was not barred by workers' compensation. Bentt v. District of Columbia Department of Employment Services, 979 A.2d 1226 (D.C. 2009).

Page 843. Please add the following note.

8. In CSX Transp., Inc. v. Hensley, 129 S.Ct. 2139 (2009), an electrician employed by the railroad brought an action under the FELA (see p. 830) for injuries arising from his workplace exposure to asbestos. In addition to damages for asbestosis, he also sought damages for fear of cancer from his exposure to asbestos. In reversing the Tennessee Court of Appeals, the Supreme Court held that the trial court was required to give a jury instruction that the plaintiff's fear of cancer claim must be "genuine and serious."

PART IV

TERMINATING THE RELATIONSHIP

CHAPTER 10

DISCHARGE

A. STATUTORY PROTECTION OF EMPLOYEES

Page 870. Please add the following notes.

2A. The Sarbanes–Oxley Act also requires that the whistleblower be a person who "provide[s] information * * * regarding any conduct which the employee reasonably believes constitutes a violation" of the pertinent laws listed in the act. The First and Fourth Circuits interpreted the term "reasonable belief" to have both a subjective and objective component. See Day v. Staples, Inc., 555 F.3d 42 (1st Cir. 2009); Welch v. Chao, 536 F.3d 269 (4th Cir. 2008). While the complaints must be made in subjective good faith and be based on objectively reasonable belief, the whistleblower need not reference a specific statute or prove actual harm. Finally, the employer's explanations given to the employee for the challenged practices are also relevant to the objective reasonableness of the belief. In Day v. Staples, the court held that "Day's beliefs were not initially reasonable as beliefs in shareholder fraud and they became less reasonable as he was given explanations."

4. The 2009 economic stimulus law (the American Recovery and Reinvestment Act) protects employees of state and local government and of contractors who whistleblow. See § 1553. The provision protects employee-whistleblowers alleging waste of stimulus funds. It covers disclosure of information reasonably believed to be evidence of gross mismanagement, gross waste, or abuse of authority. Most other federal whistleblower statutes protect only disclosure of illegal conduct or fraud.

2. CONSTITUTIONAL PROTECTIONS

Page 877. Please add the following note.

5A. At least 15 states are considering or carrying out furloughs to deal with budget deficits and nearly a million state employees are facing furloughs in the next two years. Katharine Q. Seelye, To Save Money, States Turn to Furloughs, N.Y. Times, April 24, 2009 at A1. But are furloughs legal? In February 2009, California Governor Arnold Schwarzenegger ordered two monthly furlough days for about 200,000 state employees and added a third furlough day in July 2009. Bob Egelko, Court Rules Workers' Comp Furloughs Illegal, San Francisco Chronicle, June 13, 2010 at D–2. In June 2010, the First District Court of Appeal in San Francisco ruled that the state insurance code that exempted employees of the State Compensation Insurance Fund from hiring freezes and staff cutbacks also prohibited Schwarzenegger from cutting their workweeks. Service Employees International Union, Local 1000 v. Schwarzenegger, 2010 WL 2337785 (Cal. App. 2010). About 7,900 State Compensation Insurance Fund employees who were furloughed illegally are entitled to $25 million in back pay. The court endorsed an earlier appellate court ruling that found the governor illegally furloughed about 500 lawyers and hearing officers employed by the insurance fund. California Attorneys v. Schwarzenegger, 106 Cal. Rptr.3d 702 (Cal. Ct. App. 2010). The California Supreme Court has agreed to review the legality of all of Schwarzenegger's furloughs.

New York public employee unions are challenging the constitutionality of furloughs. A federal district judge granted a preliminary injunction blocking New York Governor David Paterson from furloughing state workers. Donohue v. Paterson, 2010 WL 2178749 (N.D.N.Y.). The furlough plan would have subjected tens of thousands of public employees to a permanent 20 percent loss in salary and wages. The court held that the plaintiffs would suffer irreparable harm if no preliminary injunction were issued and that there was a substantial likelihood of success on the merits of the claim that these provisions violated the Contracts Clause of the U.S. Constitution.

Page 877. Please add after note 6.

6A. When a property interest in employment exists, what room is left for employment-at-will? In County of Dallas v. Wiland, 216 S.W.3d 344 (Tex.

2007), deputy constables were de facto terminated when the newly elected constable failed to swear them into office again. The deputy constables brought an action claiming due process violations. The court looked to the Dallas County Administrative Policies and Procedures Manual to determine whether the county conveyed a property interest to its constables. While admitting that the manual was not clear, the court concluded that the manual created an expectation of continued employment despite the clauses explicitly disavowing creation of an employment contract. The court reasoned that a "fair import" of the manual as a whole is that covered employees are not to be discharged without being given a reason they can contest. "This expectation in continued employment except for just cause, while not a contract right, as the manual expressly disavows, is nevertheless a property interest of which employees may not be deprived without due process." Interestingly the court also stated that the "important procedures for hearing and deciding grievances" established by the manual do not alone "create a property interest"; moreover, the entitlement to such procedures, without more, does not alter an employee's at-will status, thereby creating a property interest in continued employment. Do you find the court's argument regarding the unaltered status of employment at-will satisfying? Doesn't an entitlement to a procedural hearing infer some sort of right to employment beyond employment at will?

Page 877.   Please add the following to note 7.

For the status of government employment under the Equal Protection Clause, see Engquist v. Oregon Dep't of Agriculture, 553 U.S. 591 (2008), discussed supra at casebook page 225.

B.   Contractual Exceptions to At-Will Employment

1.   Breach of Contract

Page 887.   Please add the following note.

3A.   Section 2.03(a) of the Restatement Third of Employment Law (tentative draft 2009) states that "an employer must have cause for termination of (1) an unexpired agreement for a definite term of employment or (2) an agreement for an indefinite term of employment requiring cause for termination."

2.   Good Faith and Fair Dealing

Page 891.   Please add the following before note 1.

0.5.   The Restatement Third of Employment Law § 2.03 comment i (tentative draft 2009) distinguishes between the meaning of "cause" in a definite term employment agreement and in an indefinite term agreement. In a definite term agreement, unless the contract defines "cause," the word "refer[s] to misconduct, other malfeasance by the employee, or other material breach of the agreement such as, persistent neglect of duties, gross negligence, or a failure to perform the duties of the position due to a permanent disability ... [but] cause does not include changes in the economic condition of the employer." In an indefinite term agreement, "the definition of cause for termination expressly agreed to by the parties controls ... however, if the agreement is silent on the question, then ... the reasonable presumption is that the parties intended not only that the employee's misconduct, malfeasance, inability to perform the work due to permanent disability, or other material breach may constitute cause of termination but also that significant changes in the economic circumstances of the employer can supply such cause."

Page 896. Please add the following note.

6A. The Reporter's Note to Restatement Third of Employment Law comment h (tentative draft 2009) states that the Restatement does not endorse the extremely skeptical view that some courts take of indefinite term employment contracts. In some circumstances, the comment says, the law should recognize the intention of contracting parties to enter into an enforceable agreement limiting the employer's ability to terminate an employment relationship that has no definite term. The comment points to Shebar v. Sanyo Business Systems Corp., 544 A.2d 377 (N.J. 1988) in support. In *Shebar*, the court held that although an oral agreement not to be terminated except for cause did not establish a contract for lifetime employment, the promise did establish an oral agreement providing for termination only for cause.

Page 905. Please add the following note.

2A. Section 2.04, comment b of the Restatement Third of Employment Law (tentative draft 2009) discusses the efforts by some courts to fit the analysis of unilateral employer statements into the traditional offer/acceptance framework of contract law. The Restatement notes that this is awkward because "[e]mployees are rarely made aware, and even more rarely make themselves aware, of the content of these statements when they first accept employment." Thus, some courts as well as the Restatement base the enforceability of unilateral employer statements on general principles of estoppel. See, e.g., Toussaint v. Blue Cross & Blue Shield of Michigan, 292 N.W.2d 880 (Mich.1980). There, the Michigan Supreme Court focused on the benefit that accrued to an employer when it established desirable personnel policies.

Page 916. Please add the following after note 8.

9. Good faith claims do, however, reach the courts in Texas. When they do, should there be an affirmative requirement of good faith or just the lack of bad faith? Is there a difference? What if an employer erred in interpreting a clause in an employment compensation agreement, but that agreement granted broad interpretive rights to the employer as long as the employer did so absent bad faith? See, e.g., Kern v. Sitel Corp., 517 F.3d 306 (5th Cir. 2008). The court of appeals held that in interpreting an employment compensation agreement under Texas law, an employer's interpretive rights reserved by the agreement would be honored, absent a showing that the employer acted in bad faith. Although agreeing that the plaintiff's interpretation of an incentive compensation clause entitled the plaintiff to an extra $150,000 in bonus pay, the Fifth Circuit nevertheless affirmed the District Court's grant of summary judgment in favor of the employer. The Court affirmed that the employer retained final interpretive authority over the terms of the contract and did not act in bad faith. Should an employer be able to hold onto such broad interpretive rights over the terms of an employment contract?

C.   Tort Exceptions to At-Will Employment

2.   Public Policy

Page 944.   Please add the following after note 2.

2A.   Finding an articulated public policy is often difficult. In Lynn v. Wal–Mart, 280 S.W.3d 574 (Ark. App. 2008), Lynn, an employee asserted a claim of wrongful discharge in violation of public policy alleging that he was terminated for reporting inhumane workplace conditions in manufacturing facilities from which Wal–Mart buys goods. Lynn claimed his termination violated the public policy articulated in the Arkansas Deceptive Trade Practices Act, which protects the consumer from the deceptive practice of making false representation concerning the source or certification of goods. Lynn claimed Wal–Mart did just that in the company's annual report about its factory-certification process. The court affirmed a grant of summary judgment, holding that even if the court were to accept Lynn's factual allegation as true, "Lynn has simply shown no nexus between his reports of problems with the factory-certification process and any public policy of this state."

Page 947.   Please add the following before note 1.

Hanson forces the court to balance two legitimate issues: the employee's legal right or privilege and the employer's interest in regulating the workplace environment. The *Hanson* court stressed the importance of the workplace being a private property and weighed that factor heavily in ultimately ruling in favor of the employer. Would the outcome be different if the property did not belong to the employer? In Plona v. UPS, 2007 WL 509747 (N.D. Ohio 2007), an employee of UPS was terminated when he was discovered with a disassembled gun locked in his car during work. The possession of the weapon was legal but not allowed under UPS policies. The employee challenged the termination as a violation of public policy. The district court, in dismissing UPS's motion for summary judgment, stated that the Ohio constitution which gives people a right to bear arms for their defense and security creates a clear public policy. Furthermore, the district court emphasized that the important question is *where* a right is being limited. The employee's car was found in a public parking accessible to both UPS employees and others. Therefore, "punishing employees for exercising constitutional rights while outside the workplace jeopardizes public policy to a much greater degree." For a further discussion of employee guns in the workplace, see p. 119 of this supplement.

Page 947. Please add the following note.

2A. An administrative regulation issued by an agency to which the legislature has delegated authority can be the basis for a public policy tort. Plaintiff was employed by a child care facility. Her employer, seeking to earn higher profits, wanted to have a teacher-child ratio that plaintiff reasonably believed would violate a regulation issued by the state Department of Human Services. The Iowa Supreme Court affirmed a jury determination that plaintiff's discharge for contesting the employer's policies was tortious, though it reduced some of the emotional distress and punitive damages. Jasper v. H. Nizam, Inc., 764 N.W.2d 751 (Iowa 2009).

Page 948. Please add the following after note 6.

6A. In California, the Compassionate Use Act of 1996, approved by voter referendum, allows people who use marijuana for medical purposes a defense against state criminal charges of possession. Possession of marijuana, however, continues to be prohibited under federal law which lists marijuana as a highly addictive substance. United States v. Oakland Cannabis Buyers' Cooperative, 532 U.S. 483 (2001). Does the Compassionate Use Act state a clear California public policy? If so, how do these conflicting state and federal policies apply in the employment context? In Ross v. RagingWire Telecommunications, Inc., 174 P.3d 200 (Cal. 2008), a newly hired employee who suffered chronic pain from a past injury received while serving in the Air Force was required to take a drug test before starting work as a lead systems administrator. Despite showing his employer his physician's recommendation for the use of marijuana, the employee was terminated when he failed to pass a pre-employment drug test despite that drug use occurring during off-duty hours and not affecting the employee's job performance. The California Supreme Court affirmed a holding that the employee did not state an action for termination in violation of public policy, reasoning that the Compassionate Use Act was not intended to eliminate an employer's "legitimate interest in whether an employee uses the drug" and the measure was not intended to "address the respective rights and duties of employers and employees." Similarly, the Court held that the California Fair Employment and Housing Act (FEHA), which protects employees from disability-based discrimination, does not require an employer to accommodate an employee who uses marijuana for medicinal purposes. Judges Kennard and Moreno, dissenting, argued that the majority decision lacks compassion and thwarts the will of the people of California who voted for this law, also violating the employee's right not to be discriminated against under FEHA. The dissent agreed with the majority, however, that because federal law prohibits marijuana possession, the employee cannot support a claim of termination in violation of public policy.

Page 952.   Please add the following after note 2.

2A.   Furthermore, in Franklin v. Monadnock Co., 59 Cal.Rptr.3d 692 (Cal. Ct. App. 2007), the court held that public policy requires employers to provide safe and secure workplaces. The court reversed a grant of summary judgment in favor of the employer based on this holding. The plaintiff claimed that he warned his employer that a colleague was threatening to kill the plaintiff and others in the workplace. When the employer did nothing to address the situation, plaintiff reported it to authorities and was subsequently terminated. The court reasoned that plaintiff stated a claim because public policy supports encouraging employees to report credible threats of violence in the workplace.

Page 952.   Please add the following note.

4.   Plaintiff, a hospital employee, was terminated for violating a patient's confidentiality by revealing to a school teacher that a student in the teacher's class might pose a public health risk. The hospital terminated the employee for violating patient confidentiality. The appellate court agreed with the plaintiff, reversing the trial court's grant of summary judgment in favor of the hospital. The court cited numerous New Jersey statutes dealing with the protection of children as sufficient evidence of a public policy mandate. Do you agree? What about the competing public policy of patient confidentiality? Does healthcare require special public policy protection due to the special nature of the consequences? Serrano v. Christ Hosp., 945 A.2d 1288 (N.J. 2007). Compare Turner v. Memorial Med. Ctr., 911 N.E.2d 369 (Ill. 2009), where the plaintiff, a licensed respiratory therapist working for the defendant hospital, was asked to speak with a surveyor from the Joint Commission on Accreditation of Healthcare Organizations during an accreditation inspection. The plaintiff truthfully advised the surveyor that the hospital's policy on charting patient care differed from the accreditation standards, thereby endangering patient safety. After being discharged, the plaintiff sued claiming a violation of the public policy of promoting patient safety. The Supreme Court of Illinois held that "patient safety" was not a clearly mandated public policy of the state and therefore would not support a claim for retaliatory discharge.

Page 977.   Please add the following note.

4A.   The at-will model of employment allows an employer to discharge an employee for any reason or for no reason at all. What happens when actions required of an employee during the course of her employment violate her beliefs? Should an employee be allowed to refuse to do a required job function but still be allowed to keep her job if that belief is a matter of conscience for her? For example, a pharmacist at your local drug store does not believe in contraception. Should she be excused from dispensing birth control? If she refuses, does an employer have a right to fire her? States have taken various positions on this issue. Some states, like South Dakota and Mississippi, passed "conscience clause" legislation protecting pharmacists who refuse to dispense birth control. Conscience clause legislation has extended beyond its original scope of abortion and is increasingly applied to broader issues in healthcare. How do you reconcile this with the employment at-will model and an employer's right to choose its employees? There are many constitutional issues latent in this debate including freedom of religion. See James A. Sonne, Firing Thoreau: Conscience and At–Will Employment, 9 U. Pa. J. Lab. & Emp. L 235 (2007) ("contend[ing] that no protection of employee conscience is proper without a due consideration of the countervailing employer interest in at-will authority.")

D.   RETHINKING EMPLOYMENT AT-WILL

Page 978.   Please add the following note.

5A.   Consider the situation presented in Campbell v. PMI Food Equip. Group, Inc., 509 F.3d 776 (6th Cir. 2007). PMI decided to downsize a plant in Piqua, Ohio, after the expiration of its favorable tax-abatement agreement with the city. In the process, PMI terminated all 66 of the plant's hourly employees. PMI replaced the hourly workers with individuals from a temporary employment agency. The workers claimed that of the 66 hourly employees terminated 51 were over the age of 40 while the average age of the temporary workers used to replace the hourly workers was 34. The Sixth Circuit found this was not a violation of the ADEA as it was a workforce reduction that terminated 100 percent of its hourly employees regardless of whether they were over or under 40 years old. Furthermore, the hourly workers were never "replaced" as PMI did not employ the temporary workers but relied on a temp agency, an independent contractor. Do you believe the employment at-will model has worked adequately in this situation? Do you believe the hourly workers, who did have a collective bargaining agreement, should have done a better job in negotiating their rights, or has the employer been given the opportunity to side-step the law by using temporary workers?

CHAPTER 11

LEAVING A JOB

A. BREACH OF CONTRACT BY AN EMPLOYEE

Page 1005. Please renumber the existing note as note 1 and insert the following notes before "B. Post–Employment Restrictions."

2. Employers usually draft restrictive covenants to prevent former employees from using proprietary information, such as client lists and trade secrets, to establish competing businesses. Query, however, the extent to which courts will enforce such restrictions when the conduct in question falls short of outright competition. The Supreme Court of Texas held in Johnson v. Brewer & Pritchard, P.C., 73 S.W.3d 193 (Tex. 2002), that an associate at a law firm generally has no obligation to refer potential clients to that firm. The court emphasized its concern that the existence of such a duty might restrain lawyers from giving honest advice as to whether a particular firm is suited to the potential client's needs. At the same time, the court cautioned that it did not intend to "set forth a broad rule governing all employees who might divert a business opportunity from their employer without receiving any compensation or benefit in return." The court reaffirmed in particular that an employee "may not act for his future interests at the expense of his employer by using the employer's funds or employees for personal gain or by a course of conduct designed to hurt the employer." In all, *Johnson* suggests that the incidental redirection of business away from one's employer does not amount to a cognizable "competitive" act.

3. Compare the duty not to compete with the "fiduciary" duty. The fiduciary duty requires the employee not only to refrain from competing against the employer but also to act affirmatively in furtherance of the employer's interests. Most courts have declined to find any fiduciary duty for ordinary employees. In general, the fiduciary duty exists only for individuals who exercise broad managerial discretion in operating a business. See, e.g., Arrowood v. Lyon, 279 S.W.2d 801 (Ky. 1955).

4. Consider the outcome of Cameco, Inc. v. Gedicke, 724 A.2d 783 (N.J. 1999), in which the Supreme Court of New Jersey held that "employees should inform employers of their plans before establishing an independent business that might conflict with that of the employer." As a manager overseeing the shipment of Cameco's food products, Gedicke was responsible for negotiating shipment rates. While still employed by Cameco, Gedicke and two coworkers formed Newton Transportation Services, which provided the same sort of shipping services to other companies, including two of Cameco's competitors. Evidence showed that Gedicke had performed some Newton-related work at his Cameco office. The court ultimately remanded the case for resolution of a factual dispute as to whether Gedicke had breached a "duty of loyalty" to Cameco. On the one hand, the court held that "slight assistance to a direct competitor could constitute a breach of the employee's duty of loyalty." On the other hand, the court noted that "Cameco * * * [did] not contend that Newton was a direct competitor" since Newton's business consisted of transporting goods rather than producing food. To what extent does this ruling simply give an employer the power to forbid any conduct it deems "competitive"?

Page 1011.   Please add the following after note 2.

The ALI is now at work on *Restatement (Third): Employment Law.* Section 8.06, approved in 2010, says that a restrictive covenant is enforceable as long as "it is reasonably tailored in scope, geography, and time to further a protectable interest of the employer." A covenant restraining an employee from "all competition" with the employer, for instance, would likely be invalid if the employer's interest extends only to preventing the employee from particular customers as opposed to the market at large. The breadth of a covenant, however, does not in itself reduce enforceability. If an employer does business worldwide, then a worldwide prohibition on competition may well be reasonable.

Section 8.07 sets forth four categories of interests that may be protected by post-employment covenants: "confidential information," "customer relationships," "investments in the employee's reputation in the market," and "investments in the purchase of the employee's business." Confidential information includes "business plans, pricing [and] product information," and other materials that are not "generally known to the public, [with]in the employer's industry, or readily obtainable * * * through proper means." Customer relationships include typical "client" relationships, such as that between an investment manager and an investor. Protectable interests in an employee's reputation are more limited, as they tend to apply only to employees with public recognition. A television station that has spent considerable time and money in promoting the image of a news anchor, for instance, would be able to impose restrictions on the anchor's ability to leave for a competing station. Finally, the purchase of a business often turns on the purchasing employer's goal of eliminating competition from that business. The employer therefore has a protectable interest in preventing the seller, who usually becomes one of its employees, from starting a fresh competing business.

CHAPTER 12

UNEMPLOYMENT

D. UNEMPLOYMENT INSURANCE
2. THE UNEMPLOYMENT INSURANCE SYSTEM

Page 1086. Please add the following after note 1.

1A. Fifty state laws determine the length of unemployment insurance benefits and their amount. In most states, the usual length is 26 weeks. Over the last 20 years, total unemployment insurance outlays have increased 800%, from $15 billion in 1989 to $133 billion in 2009. See UI Financial Data Handbook (http://workforcesecurity.doleta.gov/unemploy/hb 394.asp). The U.S. Department of Labor estimated that the total benefits paid from all UI programs will amount to $157.1 billion in 2010, covering 16.3 million beneficiaries. Office of Unemployment Insurance, Unemployment Compensation: Federal State Partnership, U.S. Dept. of Labor, April 2010 (http://workforcesecurity.doleta.gov/unemploy/pdf/partnership.pdf). The national recession has led to the dramatic recent hike in UI outlays, heavily subsidized by the federal government. The Emergency Unemployment Compensation program of 2008 (EUC), effective from July 2008 through June 2, 2010 and 100% funded by the federal government, provided up to 34 weeks of additional benefits to eligible jobless workers in every state and up to 53 weeks in states with "high unemployment." Workers who exhaust their regular UI and EUC benefits can receive up to 20 weeks of additional benefits through the permanent federal-state Extended Benefits (EB) program (normally the cost of EB is split 50–50 between the states and the federal government but the federal government temporarily assumed 100% of the cost pursuant to the American Recovery and Reinvestment Act of 2009). As a result of the three programs, unemployed workers can be eligible for a maximum of 99 weeks of benefits averaging $335. As of July 2010, Congress had not reauthorized the federal benefits extension.

1B. The American Recovery and Reinvestment Act, P.L. 111–5 (2009), contains the Unemployment Insurance Modernization Act. In exchange for providing substantial financial assistance to state unemployment insurance programs, the law requires the states to adopt the "alternative base period" method of calculating benefits. In effect, it requires the states to consider the more recent (and presumably higher) earnings of claimants instead of the average of earnings over a longer period of time. In addition, the states must adopt at least two of the following four provisions: (1) extending benefits to employees working part-time, in contrast to many state requirements that the individual be seeking full-time work; (2) extending benefits to individuals who leave work for "compelling" family reasons, including domestic violence; (3) increasing benefits to help care for dependents; and (4) extending benefits to permanently laid off employees who are enrolled in a job training program.

3.   LEGAL ISSUES IN UNEMPLOYMENT INSURANCE

Page 1097.   Please add the following after note 3.

4.   Who is an "employee" for purposes of unemployment insurance? In a technology driven world the distinction between employee and contractor continues to blur even in sectors that have traditionally had well defined "employees." Chapter 2 makes clear that no single test defines what constitutes an "employee." In Fleece on Earth v. Department of Employment & Training, 923 A.2d 594 (Vt. 2007), the court determined that a group of knitters and sewers who worked from home at their own pace, on their own machines, and were paid by piece were employees for the purpose of assessing unemployment taxes against the buyer Fleece on Earth. In an analysis similar to the one applied to the home researchers in Donovan v. DialAmerica, supra page 401, the court reasoned that because the knitters and sewers were not free from the company's control or direction over performance of services, their work constituted employment. Isn't any independent contractor still under the control of whoever is contracting them for services? What if one of these "employees" actually sold clothing to two companies or three, would each company be assessed unemployment insurance? While not making a dispositive decision on this issue, the court in *Fleece on Earth* certainly does not foreclose this possibility.

CHAPTER 13

RETIREMENT

2.   AGE DISCRIMINATION IN EMPLOYEE BENEFIT PLANS

Page 1154.   Please add the following case before note 1.

Kentucky Retirement Systems v. EEOC

554 U.S. 135 (2008).

■ BREYER, J., delivered the opinion of the Court.

Kentucky has put in place a special retirement plan for state and county employees who occupy "[h]azardous position[s]," e.g., active duty law enforcement officers, firefighters, paramedics, and workers in correctional systems. The Plan sets forth two routes through which such an employee can become eligible for what is called "normal retirement" benefits. The first makes an employee eligible for retirement after 20 years of service. The second makes an employee eligible after only 5 years of service provided that the employee has attained the age of 55. An employee eligible under either route will receive a pension calculated in the same way: Kentucky multiplies years of service times 2.5% times final preretirement pay.

Kentucky's Plan has special provisions for hazardous position workers who become disabled but are not yet eligible for normal retirement. Where such an employee has worked for five years or became disabled in the line of duty, the employee can retire at once. In calculating that employee's benefits Kentucky will add a certain number of ("imputed") years to the employee's actual years of service. The number of imputed years equals the number of years that the disabled employee would have had to continue working in order to become eligible for normal retirement benefits, i.e., the years necessary to bring the employee up to 20 years of service or to at least 5 years of service when the employee would turn 55 (whichever number of years is lower). Thus, if an employee with 17 years of service becomes disabled at age 48, the Plan adds 3 years and calculates the benefits as if the employee had completed 20 years of service. If an employee with 17 years of service becomes disabled at age 54, the Plan adds 1 year and calculates the benefits as if the employee had retired at age 55 with 18 years of service.

The Plan also imposes a ceiling on imputed years equal to the number of years the employee has previously worked (i.e., an employee who has worked eight years cannot receive more than eight additional imputed years); it provides for a certain minimum payment; and it contains various other details, none of which is challenged here.

Charles Lickteig, a hazardous position worker in the Jefferson County Sheriff's Department, became eligible for retirement at age 55, continued to work, became disabled, and then retired at age 61. The Plan calculated his annual pension on the basis of his actual years of service (18 years) times 2.5% times his final annual pay. Because Lickteig became disabled after he had already become eligible for normal retirement benefits, the Plan did not impute any additional years for purposes of the calculation.

Lickteig complained of age discrimination to the Equal Employment Opportunity Commission (EEOC); and the EEOC then brought this age discrimination lawsuit against the Commonwealth of Kentucky, Kentucky's Plan administrator, and other state entities. The EEOC pointed out that, if Lickteig had become disabled before he reached the age of 55, the Plan, in calculating Lickteig's benefits would have imputed a number of additional years. And the EEOC argued that the Plan failed to impute years solely because Lickteig became disabled after he reached age 55.

* * *

The ADEA forbids an employer to "fail or refuse to hire or to discharge any individual or otherwise discriminate against any individual with respect to his compensation, terms, conditions, or privileges of employment, because of such individual's age."

* * *

In Hazen Paper Co. v. Biggins, 507 U.S. 604 (1993), the Court considered a disparate treatment claim that an employer had unlawfully dismissed a 62–year–old employee with over 9 1/2 years of service in order to avoid paying pension benefits that would have vested after 10 years. The Court held that, without more evidence of intent, the ADEA would not forbid dismissal of the claim. A dismissal based on pension status was not a dismissal "because ... of age." Of course, pension status depended upon years of service, and years of service typically go hand in hand with age. But the two concepts were nonetheless "analytically distinct." An employer could easily "take account of one while ignoring the other." And the dismissal in question, if based purely upon pension status (related to years of service), would not embody the evils that led Congress to enact the ADEA in the first place: The dismissal was not based on a "prohibited stereotype" of older workers, did not produce any "attendant stigma" to those workers, and was not "the result of an inaccurate and denigrating generalization about age."

At the same time, *Hazen Paper* indicated that discrimination on the basis of pension status could sometimes be unlawful under the ADEA, in particular where pension status served as a "proxy for age." Suppose, for example, an employer "target[ed] employees with a particular pension status on the assumption that these employees are likely to be older." In such a case, *Hazen Paper* suggested, age, not pension status, would have "actually motivated" the employer's decisionmaking. *Hazen Paper* also left open "the special case where an employee is about to vest in pension benefits as a result of his age, rather than years of service." We here consider a variation on this "special case" theme.

Kentucky's Plan turns normal pension eligibility either upon the employee's having attained 20 years of service alone or upon the employees having attained 5 years of service and reached the age of 55. The ADEA permits an employer to condition pension eligibility upon age. Thus we must decide whether a plan that (1) lawfully makes age in part a condition of pension eligibility, and (2) treats workers differently in light of their pension status, (3) automatically discriminates because of age. The Government argues "yes." But, following *Hazen Paper's* approach, we come to a different conclusion. In particular, the following circumstances, taken together, convince us that, in this particular instance, differences in treatment were not "actually motivated" by age.

First, as a matter of pure logic, age and pension status remain "analytically distinct" concepts. That is to say, one can easily conceive of decisions that are actually made "because of" pension status and not age, even where pension status is itself based on age. Suppose, for example that an employer pays all retired workers a pension, retirement eligibility turns on age, say 65, and a 70–year–old worker retires. Nothing in language or in logic prevents one from concluding that the employer has begun to pay the worker a pension, not because the worker is over 65, but simply because the worker has retired.

Second, several background circumstances eliminate the possibility that pension status, though analytically distinct from age, nonetheless serves as a "proxy for age" in Kentucky's Plan. We consider not an individual employment decision, but a set of complex systemwide rules. These systemic rules involve, not wages, but pensions—a benefit that the ADEA treats somewhat more flexibly and leniently in respect to age. And the specific benefit at issue here is offered to all hazardous position workers on the same nondiscriminatory terms ex ante. That is to say, every such employee, when hired, is promised disability retirement benefits should he become disabled prior to the time that he is eligible for normal retirement benefits.

Furthermore, Congress has otherwise approved of programs that calculate permanent disability benefits using a formula that expressly takes account of age. For example, the Social Security Administration now uses such a formula in calculating Social Security Disability Insurance benefits. And until (and in some cases after) 1984, federal employees received permanent disability benefits based on a formula that, in certain circumstances, did not just consider age, but effectively imputed years of service only to those disabled workers younger than 60.

Third, there is a clear non-age-related rationale for the disparity here at issue. The manner in which Kentucky calculates disability retirement benefits is in every important respect but one identical to the manner in which Kentucky calculates normal retirement benefits. The one significant difference consists of the fact that the Plan imputes additional years of service to disabled individuals. But the Plan imputes only those years needed to bring the disabled worker's years of service to 20 or to the number of years that the individual would have worked had he worked to age 55. The disability rules clearly track Kentucky's normal retirement rules.

It is obvious, then, that the whole purpose of the disability rules is, as Kentucky claims, to treat a disabled worker as though he had become disabled after, rather than before, he had become eligible for normal retirement benefits. Age factors into the disability calculation only because the normal retirement rules themselves permissibly include age as a consideration. No one seeking to help disabled workers in the way that Kentucky's rules seek to help those workers would care whether Kentucky's normal system turned eligibility in part upon age or upon other, different criteria.

* * *

It bears emphasizing that our opinion in no way unsettles the rule that a statute or policy that facially discriminates based on age suffices to show disparate treatment under the ADEA. We are dealing today with the quite special case of differential treatment based on pension status, where pension status—with the explicit blessing of the ADEA—itself turns, in part, on age. Further, the rule we adopt today for dealing with this sort of case is clear: Where an employer adopts a pension plan that includes age as a factor, and that employer then treats employees differently based on pension status, a plaintiff, to state a disparate treatment claim under the ADEA, must adduce sufficient evidence to show that the differential treatment was "actually motivated" by age, not pension status. And our discussion of the factors that lead us to conclude that the Government has failed to make the requisite showing in this case provides an indication of what a plaintiff might show in other cases to meet his burden of proving that differential treatment based on pension status is in fact discrimination "because of" age.

* * *

The judgment of the Court of Appeals is reversed.

■ JUSTICE KENNEDY, with whom JUSTICE SCALIA, JUSTICE GINSBURG, and JUSTICE ALITO join, dissenting.

The Court today ignores established rules for interpreting and enforcing one of the most important statutes Congress has enacted to protect the Nation's work force from age discrimination, the Age Discrimination in Employment Act of 1967. That Act prohibits employment actions that "discriminate against any individual with respect to his compensation, terms, conditions, or privileges of employment, because of such individual's age." In recent years employers and employees alike have been advised by this Court, by most Courts of Appeals, and by the agency charged with enforcing the Act, the Equal Employment Opportunity Commission, that the most straightforward reading of the statute is the correct one: When an employer makes age a factor in an employee benefit plan in a formal, facial, deliberate, and explicit manner, to the detriment of older employees, this is a violation of the Act. Disparate treatment on the basis of age is prohibited unless some exemption or defense provided in the Act applies.

The Court today undercuts this basic framework. In doing so it puts the Act and its enforcement on a wrong course. The decision of the en banc panel of the Court of Appeals for the Sixth Circuit, which the Court reverses, brought that Circuit's case law into line with that of its sister Circuits. By embracing the approach rejected by the en banc panel and all other Courts of Appeals that have addressed this issue, this Court creates unevenness in administration, unpredictability in litigation, and uncertainty as to employee rights once thought well settled. These consequences, and the Court's errors in interpreting the statute and our cases, require this respectful dissent.

Even were the Court correct that Kentucky's facially discriminatory disability benefits plan can be justified by a proper motive, the employer's own submission to us reveals that the plan's discriminatory classification rests upon a stereotypical assumption that itself violates the Act and the Court's own analytical framework.

As a threshold matter, all should concede that the paradigm offered to justify the statute is a powerful one: The young police officer or firefighter with a family is disabled in the heroic performance of his or her duty. Disability payments are increased to account for unworked years of service. What the Court overlooks, however, is that a 61–year–old officer or firefighter who is disabled in the same heroic action receives, in many instances, a lower payment and for one reason alone: By explicit command of Kentucky's disability plan age is an express disadvantage in calculating the disability payment.

This is a straightforward act of discrimination on the basis of age. Though the Commonwealth is entitled by the law, in some instances, to defend an age-based differential as cost justified, that has yet to be established here. What an employer cannot do, and what the Court ought not to do, is to pretend that this explicit discrimination based on age is somehow consistent with the broad statutory and regulatory prohibition against disparate treatment based on age.

* * *

Consider two covered workers, one 45 and one 55, both with five years of service with the Commonwealth and an annual salary of $60,000. If we assume both become disabled in the same accident, the 45–year–old will be entitled to receive $1,250 in monthly benefits; the 55–year–old will receive $625, just half as much. The benefit disparity results from the Commonwealth's decision, under the disability retirement formula, to credit the 45–year–old with 5 years of unworked service (thereby increasing the appliable years-service-multipler to 10 years), while the 55–year–old's benefits are based only on actual years of service (5 years). In that instance age is the only factor that accounts for the disparate treatment.

True, age is not a factor that reduces benefits in every case. If a worker has accumulated 20 years of service with the Commonwealth before he or she becomes disabled, age plays no role in the benefits calculation. But there is no question that, in many cases, a disabled worker over the age of 55 who has accumulated fewer than 20 years of service receives a lower monthly stipend than otherwise similarly situated workers who are under 55. The Court concludes this result is something other than discrimination on the basis of age only by ignoring the statute and our past opinions.

* * *

At a minimum the Court should not cite *Hazen Paper* to support what it now holds. Its conclusion that no disparate-treatment violation has been established here conflicts with the longstanding rule in ADEA cases. The rule-confirmed by the quoted text in *Hazen Paper*—is that once the plaintiff establishes that a policy discriminates on its face, no additional proof of a less-than-benign motive for the challenged employment action is required. For if the plan discriminates on its face, it is obvious that decisions made pursuant to the plan are "actually motivated" by age. The EEOC (or the employee) must prevail unless the employer can justify its action under one of the enumerated statutory defenses or exemptions.

* * *

As explained in this dissent, Kentucky's disability retirement plan violates the ADEA, an Act intended to promote the interests of older Americans. Yet it is no small irony that it does so, at least in part, because the Commonwealth's normal retirement plan treats older workers in a particularly generous fashion. Kentucky allows its employees to retire at the age of 55 if they have accumulated only five years of service. But for this provision, which links age and years of service in a way that benefits older workers, pension eligibility would be a function solely of tenure, not age. Accordingly, this case would be more like *Hazen Paper* and the EEOC's case would be much weaker. Similarly, as the Court notes, Kentucky could avoid any problems by not imputing unworked years of service to any disabled workers, old and young alike. Neither change to the plan would result in more generous treatment for older workers. The only difference would be that, under the first example, older workers would lose the option of early retirement, and, under the second, younger workers would see their benefits cut. These are not the only possible remedies—the Commonwealth could impute unworked years of service to all employees forced into retirement on account of a disability regardless of age.

The Court's desire to avoid construing the ADEA in a way that encourages the Commonwealth to eliminate its early retirement program or to reduce benefits to the policemen and firefighters who are covered under the disability plan is understandable. But, under our precedents, " '[a] benefit that is part and parcel of the employment relationship may not be doled out in a discriminatory fashion, even if the employer would be free . . . not to provide the benefit at all.' " If Kentucky's facially discriminatory plan is good public policy, the answer is not for this Court to ignore its precedents and the plain text of the statute.

For these reasons, in my view, the judgment of the Court of Appeals should be affirmed and the case remanded for a determination whether the State can assert a cost-justification defense.

B. PRIVATE PENSIONS

2. ERISA

Page 1167. Please add the following after note 3.

3A. William Kennedy named his wife Liv Kennedy as beneficiary of his DuPont Corporation pension plan. When, 20 years after the designation, William and Liv divorced, Liv waived any right to William's pension. But William never corrected the designation of Liv as beneficiary in the papers he had filed at the company. Therefore, on William's death, DuPont paid Liv the benefits he had earned. William and Liv's daughter Kari Kennedy, executor of her father's estate, sued, saying that because her mother had given up any right to his pension assets, the money should have gone to the estate. The Supreme Court said no. Because the plan documents control, they obligated William to change in writing his designation of a beneficiary, and therefore Liv can keep the money. Kennedy v. Plan Adm'r for DuPont Sav. & Inv. Plan, ___ U.S. ___, 129 S.Ct. 865 (2009).

Page 1173. Please add the following note.

2A. How difficult should it be under ERISA for an employer to eliminate employee benefit plans? To what extent does such an employer have fiduciary obligations to make fair changes or reductions in a plan? As discussed previously, an employer has no obligations under ERISA to provide pension plan benefits. However, should an employer choose to provide benefits, ERISA governs their administration. In Beck v. PACE Int'l Union, 551 U.S. 96 (2007), plan participants sued a bankrupt employer for breach of fiduciary duty under ERISA after the distressed company decided to terminate pension plans by purchasing annuities. Plan participants claimed the employer failed in its fiduciary duties when it did not consider a proposed plan to merge the pension benefits plan into a multiemployer plan advocated by the union. The Supreme Court held that merger into a multiemployer plan is not a permissible method of terminating a single-employer defined-benefit plan.

Similarly, once an employer does set up a certain type of ERISA governed pension plan, should an employer be completely free to change the plan? In Register v. PNC Financial Services Group, Inc., 477 F.3d 56 (3d Cir. 2007), PNC employees challenged PNC's conversion of its pension plan from a traditional defined benefit plan to a cash balance plan. Although, the accrual system of the cash benefit plan resulted in unequal disadvantage to older workers, the Fourth Circuit held that the change to a cash benefit plan was permissible as it did not violate ERISA's anti-discrimination provisions because the employee's benefit accrual was reduced for all workers, not just for older ones.

Page 1175. Please add the following note.

7. In LaRue v. DeWolff, Boberg & Assoc., Inc., 458 F.3d 359 (4th Cir. 2006), the Fourth Circuit held, contrary to the wishes of the Secretary of Labor, that an individual worker does not have a claim for breach of fiduciary duty under ERISA. James LaRue sought to exercise his option to make certain changes in his ERISA governed 401(k) retirement plan. His employer, DeWolff, failed to make his requested changes, allegedly costing LaRue about $150,000. The Fourth Circuit held that a broad reading of section 502(a)(2) "would necessarily transform every purely individual claim for breach of fiduciary duty into a 'plan loss.' Such an expansive view of fiduciary liability would lead to its own parade of horribles..." The Third, Fifth, Sixth, and Seventh Circuits disagreed, allowing subsets of plan beneficiaries to sue for breach of fiduciary duty under ERISA. The Supreme Court did not think it would lead to such a "parade of horribles" either, reversing the Fourth Circuit and finding in Mr. LaRue's favor. 552 U.S. 248 (2008). The Court reasoned that although the language of section 502(a)(2) does not distinguish between an individual remedy for injuries from plan injuries, the provision does authorize recovery for fiduciary breaches that impair the value of plan assets in a participant's individual account.

Page 1182.   Please add the following note.

2A.   Is it appropriate to have ERISA benefits administrators also fund the benefit awards? Does such a structural combination contain an inherent conflict of interests making any decision by such a plan administrator subject to greater judicial review under Firestone Tire & Rubber v. Bruch, casebook page 1190? Plaintiff Wanda Glenn, a Sears Roebuck employee, had a heart disorder. MetLife, both administering and funding the Sears Roebuck plan, first granted Ms. Glenn 24 months of disability benefits. MetLife encouraged her to apply for Social Security disability benefits, see casebook page 857, which she received based on a determination that she could not work. MetLife then found her capable of doing sedentary work and denied further benefits. The Supreme Court affirmed the Sixth Circuit's decision that MetLife's denial of benefits should be overturned, in part because of MetLife's conflict of interest. Justices Scalia and Thomas dissented and Justice Kennedy dissented in part. Metropolitan Life Ins. Co. v. Glenn, 552 U.S. 1161 (2008).

Page 1194.   Please add the following note.

10.   The Supreme Court held in Conkright v. Frommert, 130 S.Ct. 1640 (2010), that a plan administrator who makes an "honest mistake" in interpreting a retirement plan is not automatically disqualified from exercising discretion in future interpretations. Years before the dispute arose, Frommert and other plaintiff employees had left Xerox and collected lump-sum payments from the plan. When the plaintiffs subsequently rejoined the company and resumed accruing benefits, Conkright faced the task of deducting the lump-sum payments from future distributions so as to avoid double-paying the plaintiffs for their earlier period of employment. Conkright eventually adopted a "phantom account" method for calculating the deductions; the essence of the method was to account for the time value of the lump-sum payments. The Second Circuit, however, invalidated the approach for being an "arbitrary and capricious" interpretation of the plan and remanded the case to the district court. Conkright then presented to the district court an alternative method for accounting for the time value of the payments, but the district court rejected the suggested approach in favor of a formula that did not account for the time value of money at all. The Supreme Court criticized the district court for taking a "one-strike-and-you're-out" approach. Emphasizing ERISA's "careful balancing" of employees' rights with the practical demands of plan administration, the Court found that "the interests in efficiency, predictability, and uniformity—and the manner in which they are promoted by deference to a reasonable plan construction by administrators—do not suddenly disappear simply because a plan administrator has made a single honest mistake."

The Supreme Court has now granted certiorari in another case that raises issues overlapping with *Conkright*. After CIGNA Corporation converted its traditional defined benefit pension plan to a cash balance plan, it gave plan participants a summary plan description, known as an SPD. The

U.S. District Court held that the SPD misrepresented the terms of the plan. CIGNA said that the plaintiffs (a class of 26,000 plan participants was certified) had demonstrated "likely harm" and that CIGNA had failed to establish that its error had been harmless. Amara v. CIGNA Corp., 348 Fed.Appx. 627 (2d Cir. 2009), cert. granted, 130 S.Ct. ___ (2010).

Page 1210.   Please add the following note.

8.   The Ninth Circuit held in Doyle v. City of Medford, 606 F.3d 667 (9th Cir. 2010), that retirement benefits constitute a property interest only if those benefits are defined with sufficient clarity. The Oregon legislature had passed a statute providing that all cities "shall, insofar as and to the extent possible," provide retirement benefits to certain civil servants. Shortly thereafter, Medford passed its own implementing resolution, which listed health care among the benefits to be provided. Although Medford honored its commitment for several years, it eventually removed the health care benefits. When Doyle sued on the ground that the removal amounted to a deprivation of property in violation of due process, the Ninth Circuit found that the "insofar as and to the extent possible" provision of the Oregon statute created obligations that were "too indeterminate" to be enforceable. The Ninth Circuit emphasized that "[o]nly if the governing statute compels a result upon compliance with certain criteria, none of which involve[s] the exercise of discretion by the reviewing body, does it create a constitutionally protected property interest."

APPENDIX A

GENETIC INFORMATION NONDISCRIMINATION ACT OF 2008

P.L. 110–233, 122 Stat. 881 (2008).

* * *

TITLE II—PROHIBITING EMPLOYMENT DISCRIMINATION ON THE BASIS OF GENETIC INFORMATION

§ 201. DEFINITIONS

* * *

(4) GENETIC INFORMATION—

(A) IN GENERAL—The term "genetic information" means, with respect to any individual, information about—

(i) such individual's genetic tests,

(ii) the genetic tests of family members of such individual, and

(iii) the manifestation of a disease or disorder in family members of such individual.

(B) INCLUSION OF GENETIC SERVICES AND PARTICIPATION IN GENETIC RESEARCH—Such term includes, with respect to any individual, any request for, or receipt of, genetic services, or participation in clinical research which includes genetic services, by such individual or any family member of such individual.

(C) EXCLUSIONS—The term "genetic information" shall not include information about the sex or age of any individual.

(5) GENETIC MONITORING—The term "genetic monitoring" means the periodic examination of employees to evaluate acquired modifications to their genetic material, such as chromosomal damage or evidence of increased occurrence of mutations, that may have developed in the course of employment due to exposure to toxic substances in the workplace, in order to identify, evaluate, and respond to the effects of or control adverse environmental exposures in the workplace.

(6) GENETIC SERVICES—The term "genetic services" means—

(A) a genetic test;

(B) genetic counseling (including obtaining, interpreting, or assessing genetic information); or

(C) genetic education.

(7) GENETIC TEST—

(A) IN GENERAL—The term "genetic test" means an analysis of human DNA, RNA, chromosomes, proteins, or metabolites, that detects genotypes, mutations, or chromosomal changes.

(B) EXCEPTIONS The term "genetic test" does not mean an analysis of proteins or metabolites that does not detect genotypes, mutations, or chromosomal changes.

§ 202. EMPLOYER PRACTICES.

(a) Discrimination Based on Genetic Information—It shall be an unlawful employment practice for an employer—

(1) to fail or refuse to hire, or to discharge, any employee, or otherwise to discriminate against any employee with respect to the compensation, terms, conditions, or privileges of employment of the employee, because of genetic information with respect to the employee; or

(2) to limit, segregate, or classify the employees of the employer in any way that would deprive or tend to deprive any employee of employment opportunities or otherwise adversely affect the status of the employee as an employee, because of genetic information with respect to the employee.

(b) Acquisition of Genetic Information—It shall be an unlawful employment practice for an employer to request, require, or purchase genetic information with respect to an employee or a family member of the employee except—

(1) where an employer inadvertently requests or requires family medical history of the employee or family member of the employee;

(2) where—

(A) health or genetic services are offered by the employer, including such services offered as part of a wellness program;

(B) the employee provides prior, knowing, voluntary, and written authorization;

(C) only the employee (or family member if the family member is receiving genetic services) and the licensed health care professional or board certified genetic counselor involved in providing such services receive individually identifiable information concerning the results of such services; and

(D) any individually identifiable genetic information provided under subparagraph (C) in connection with the services provided under subparagraph (A) is only available for purposes of such services and shall not be disclosed to the employer except in aggregate terms that do not disclose the identity of specific employees;

(3) where an employer requests or requires family medical history from the employee to comply with the certification provisions of section 103 of the Family and Medical Leave Act of 1993 (29 U.S.C. 2613) or such requirements under State family and medical leave laws;

(4) where an employer purchases documents that are commercially and publicly available (including newspapers, magazines, periodicals, and books, but not including medical databases or court records) that include family medical history;

(5) where the information involved is to be used for genetic monitoring of the biological effects of toxic substances in the workplace, but only if—

(A) the employer provides written notice of the genetic monitoring to the employee;

(B) (i) the employee provides prior, knowing, voluntary, and written authorization; or

(ii) the genetic monitoring is required by Federal or State law;

(C) the employee is informed of individual monitoring results;

(D) the monitoring is in compliance with—

(i) any Federal genetic monitoring regulations, including any such regulations that may be promulgated by the Secretary of Labor pursuant to the Occupational Safety and Health Act of 1970 (29 U.S.C. 651 et seq.), the Federal Mine Safety and Health Act of 1977 (30 U.S.C. 801 et seq.), or the Atomic Energy Act of 1954 (42 U.S.C. 2011 et seq.); or

(ii) State genetic monitoring regulations, in the case of a State that is implementing genetic monitoring regulations under the authority of the Occupational Safety and Health Act of 1970 (29 U.S.C. 651 et seq.); and

(E) the employer, excluding any licensed health care professional or board certified genetic counselor that is involved in the genetic monitoring program, receives the results of the monitoring only in aggregate terms that do not disclose the identity of specific employees; or

(6) where the employer conducts DNA analysis for law enforcement purposes as a forensic laboratory or for purposes of human remains identification, and requests or requires genetic information of such employer's employees, but only to the extent that such genetic

information is used for analysis of DNA identification markers for quality control to detect sample contamination.

(c) Preservation of Protections—In the case of information to which any of paragraphs (1) through (6) of subsection (b) applies, such information may not be used in violation of paragraph (1) or (2) of subsection (a) or treated or disclosed in a manner that violates section 206.

* * *

§ 206. CONFIDENTIALITY OF GENETIC INFORMATION.

(a) Treatment of Information as Part of Confidential Medical Record— If an employer, employment agency, labor organization, or joint labor-management committee possesses genetic information about an employee or member, such information shall be maintained on separate forms and in separate medical files and be treated as a confidential medical record of the employee or member. An employer, employment agency, labor organization, or joint labor-management committee shall be considered to be in compliance with the maintenance of information requirements of this subsection with respect to genetic information subject to this subsection that is maintained with and treated as a confidential medical record under section 102(d)(3)(B) of the Americans With Disabilities Act (42 U.S.C. 12112(d)(3)(B)).

(b) Limitation on Disclosure—An employer, employment agency, labor organization, or joint labor-management committee shall not disclose genetic information concerning an employee or member except—

(1) to the employee or member of a labor organization (or family member if the family member is receiving the genetic services) at the written request of the employee or member of such organization;

(2) to an occupational or other health researcher if the research is conducted in compliance with the regulations and protections provided for under part 46 of title 45, Code of Federal Regulations;

(3) in response to an order of a court, except that—

(A) the employer, employment agency, labor organization, or joint labor-management committee may disclose only the genetic information expressly authorized by such order; and

(B) if the court order was secured without the knowledge of the employee or member to whom the information refers, the employer, employment agency, labor organization, or joint labor-management committee shall inform the employee or member of the court order and any genetic information that was disclosed pursuant to such order;

(4) to government officials who are investigating compliance with this title if the information is relevant to the investigation;

(5) to the extent that such disclosure is made in connection with the employee's compliance with the certification provisions of section 103 of the Family and Medical Leave Act of 1993 (29 U.S.C. 2613) or such requirements under State family and medical leave laws; or

(6) to a Federal, State, or local public health agency only with regard to information that is described in section 201(4)(A)(iii) and that concerns a contagious disease that presents an imminent hazard of death or life-threatening illness, and that the employee whose family member or family members is or are the subject of a disclosure under this paragraph is notified of such disclosure.

(c) Relationship to HIPAA Regulations—With respect to the regulations promulgated by the Secretary of Health and Human Services under part C of title XI of the Social Security Act (42 U.S.C. 1320d et seq.) and section 264 of the Health Insurance Portability and Accountability Act of 1996 (42 U.S.C. 1320d–2 note), this title does not prohibit a covered entity under such regulations from any use or disclosure of health information that is authorized for the covered entity under such regulations. The previous sentence does not affect the authority of such Secretary to modify such regulations.

§ 207. REMEDIES AND ENFORCEMENT.

(a) Employees Covered by Title VII of the Civil Rights Act of 1964—

(1) IN GENERAL—The powers, procedures, and remedies provided in sections 705, 706, 707, 709, 710, and 711 of the Civil Rights Act of 1964 (42 U.S.C. 2000e–4 et seq.) to the Commission, the Attorney General, or any person, alleging a violation of title VII of that Act (42 U.S.C. 2000e et seq.) shall be the powers, procedures, and remedies this title provides to the Commission, the Attorney General, or any person, respectively, alleging an unlawful employment practice in violation of this title against an employee described in section 201(2)(A)(i), except as provided in paragraphs (2) and (3).

(2) COSTS AND FEES—The powers, remedies, and procedures provided in subsections (b) and (c) of section 722 of the Revised Statutes of the United States (42 U.S.C. 1988), shall be powers, remedies, and procedures this title provides to the Commission, the Attorney General, or any person, alleging such a practice.

(3) DAMAGES—The powers, remedies, and procedures provided in section 1977A of the Revised Statutes of the United States (42 U.S.C. 1981a), including the limitations contained in subsection (b)(3) of such section 1977A, shall be powers, remedies, and procedures this title provides to the Commission, the Attorney General, or any person, alleging such a practice (not an employment practice specifically ex-

cluded from coverage under section 1977A(a)(1) of the Revised Statutes of the United States).

* * *

(f) Prohibition Against Retaliation—No person shall discriminate against any individual because such individual has opposed any act or practice made unlawful by this title or because such individual made a charge, testified, assisted, or participated in any manner in an investigation, proceeding, or hearing under this title. The remedies and procedures otherwise provided for under this section shall be available to aggrieved individuals with respect to violations of this subsection.

(g) Definition—In this section, the term "Commission" means the Equal Employment Opportunity Commission.

§ 208.   DISPARATE IMPACT.

(a) General Rule—Notwithstanding any other provision of this Act, "disparate impact", as that term is used in section 703(k) of the Civil Rights Act of 1964 (42 U.S.C. 2000e–2(k)), on the basis of genetic information does not establish a cause of action under this Act.

* * *

§ 209.   CONSTRUCTION.

(a) In General—Nothing in this title shall be construed to—

(1) limit the rights or protections of an individual under any other Federal or State statute that provides equal or greater protection to an individual than the rights or protections provided for under this title, including the protections of an individual under the Americans with Disabilities Act of 1990 (42 U.S.C. 12101 et seq.) (including coverage afforded to individuals under section 102 of such Act (42 U.S.C. 12112)), or under the Rehabilitation Act of 1973 (29 U.S.C. 701 et seq.);

* * *

(4) limit or expand the protections, rights, or obligations of employees or employers under applicable workers' compensation laws;

(5) limit the authority of a Federal department or agency to conduct or sponsor occupational or other health research that is conducted in compliance with the regulations contained in part 46 of title 45, Code of Federal Regulations (or any corresponding or similar regulation or rule);

(6) limit the statutory or regulatory authority of the Occupational Safety and Health Administration or the Mine Safety and Health

Administration to promulgate or enforce workplace safety and health laws and regulations; or

* * *

(1) with respect to such an individual or family member of an individual who is a pregnant woman, include genetic information of any fetus carried by such pregnant woman; and

(2) with respect to an individual or family member utilizing an assisted reproductive technology, include genetic information of any embryo legally held by the individual or family member.

(c) Relation to Authorities Under Title I—With respect to a group health plan, or a health insurance issuer offering group health insurance coverage in connection with a group health plan, this title does not prohibit any activity of such plan or issuer that is authorized for the plan or issuer under any provision of law referred to in clauses (i) through (iv) of subsection (a)(2)(B).

§ 210. MEDICAL INFORMATION THAT IS NOT GENETIC INFORMATION.

An employer, employment agency, labor organization, or joint labor-management committee shall not be considered to be in violation of this title based on the use, acquisition, or disclosure of medical information that is not genetic information about a manifested disease, disorder, or pathological condition of an employee or member, including a manifested disease, disorder, or pathological condition that has or may have a genetic basis.

§ 211. REGULATIONS.

Not later than 1 year after the date of enactment of this title, the Commission shall issue final regulations to carry out this title.

* * *

§ 213. EFFECTIVE DATE.

This title takes effect on the date that is 18 months after the date of enactment of this Act.

ADA AMENDMENTS ACT OF 2008

P.L. 110–325 (2008).

SECTION 1.   SHORT TITLE.

This Act may be cited as the "ADA Amendments Act of 2008".

SEC. 2.   FINDINGS AND PURPOSES.

(a) FINDINGS.—Congress finds that—

(1) in enacting the Americans with Disabilities Act of 1990 (ADA), Congress intended that the Act "provide a clear and comprehensive national mandate for the elimination of discrimination against individuals with disabilities" and provide broad coverage;

(2) in enacting the ADA, Congress recognized that physical and mental disabilities in no way diminish a person's right to fully participate in all aspects of society, but that people with physical or mental disabilities are frequently precluded from doing so because of prejudice, antiquated attitudes, or the failure to remove societal and institutional barriers;

(3) while Congress expected that the definition of disability under the ADA would be interpreted consistently with how courts had applied the definition of a handicapped individual under the Rehabilitation Act of 1973, that expectation has not been fulfilled;

(4) the holdings of the Supreme Court in Sutton v. United Air Lines, Inc., 527 U.S. 471 (1999) and its companion cases have narrowed the broad scope of protection intended to be afforded by the ADA, thus eliminating protection for many individuals whom Congress intended to protect;

(5) the holding of the Supreme Court in Toyota Motor Manufacturing, Kentucky, Inc. v. Williams, 534 U.S. 184 (2002) further narrowed the broad scope of protection intended to be afforded by the ADA;

(6) as a result of these Supreme Court cases, lower courts have incorrectly found in individual cases that people with a range of substantially limiting impairments are not people with disabilities;

(7) in particular, the Supreme Court, in the case of Toyota Motor Manufacturing, Kentucky, Inc. v. Williams, 534 U.S. 184 (2002), interpreted the term "substantially limits" to require a greater degree of limitation than was intended by Congress; and

(8) Congress finds that the current Equal Employment Opportunity Commission ADA regulations defining the term "substantially lim-

157

its" as "significantly restricted" are inconsistent with congressional intent, by expressing too high a standard.

(b) PURPOSES.—The purposes of this Act are—

(1) to carry out the ADA's objectives of providing "a clear and comprehensive national mandate for the elimination of discrimination" and "clear, strong, consistent, enforceable standards addressing discrimination" by reinstating a broad scope of protection to be available under the ADA;

(2) to reject the requirement enunciated by the Supreme Court in Sutton v. United Air Lines, Inc., 527 U.S. 471 (1999) and its companion cases that whether an impairment substantially limits a major life activity is to be determined with reference to the ameliorative effects of mitigating measures;

(3) to reject the Supreme Court's reasoning in Sutton v. United Air Lines, Inc., 527 U.S. 471 (1999) with regard to coverage under the third prong of the definition of disability and to reinstate the reasoning of the Supreme Court in School Board of Nassau County v. Arline, 480 U.S. 273 (1987) which set forth a broad view of the third prong of the definition of handicap under the Rehabilitation Act of 1973;

(4) to reject the standards enunciated by the Supreme Court in Toyota Motor Manufacturing, Kentucky, Inc. v. Williams, 534 U.S. 184 (2002), that the terms "substantially" and "major" in the definition of disability under the ADA "need to be interpreted strictly to create a demanding standard for qualifying as disabled," and that to be substantially limited in performing a major life activity under the ADA "an individual must have an impairment that prevents or severely restricts the individual from doing activities that are of central importance to most people's daily lives";

(5) to convey congressional intent that the standard created by the Supreme Court in the case of Toyota Motor Manufacturing, Kentucky, Inc. v. Williams, 534 U.S. 184 (2002) for "substantially limits", and applied by lower courts in numerous decisions, has created an inappropriately high level of limitation necessary to obtain coverage under the ADA, to convey that it is the intent of Congress that the primary object of attention in cases brought under the ADA should be whether entities covered under the ADA have complied with their obligations, and to convey that the question of whether an individual's impairment is a disability under the ADA should not demand extensive analysis; and

(6) to express Congress' expectation that the Equal Employment Opportunity Commission will revise that portion of its current regulations that defines the term "substantially limits" as "significantly

restricted" to be consistent with this Act, including the amendments made by this Act.

* * *

SEC. 4. DISABILITY DEFINED AND RULES OF CONSTRUCTION.

(a) DEFINITION OF DISABILITY.—Section 3 of the Americans with Disabilities Act of 1990 (42 U.S.C. 12102) is amended to read as follows:

"SEC. 3. DEFINITION OF DISABILITY.

"As used in this Act:

"(1) DISABILITY.—The term 'disability' means, with respect to an individual—

"(A) a physical or mental impairment that substantially limits one or more major life activities of such individual;

"(B) a record of such an impairment; or

"(C) being regarded as having such an impairment (as described in paragraph (3)).

"(2) MAJOR LIFE ACTIVITIES.—

"(A) IN GENERAL.—For purposes of paragraph (1), major life activities include, but are not limited to, caring for oneself, performing manual tasks, seeing, hearing, eating, sleeping, walking, standing, lifting, bending, speaking, breathing, learning, reading, concentrating, thinking, communicating, and working.

"(B) MAJOR BODILY FUNCTIONS.—For purposes of paragraph (1), a major life activity also includes the operation of a major bodily function, including but not limited to, functions of the immune system, normal cell growth, digestive, bowel, bladder, neurological, brain, respiratory, circulatory, endocrine, and reproductive functions.

"(3) REGARDED AS HAVING SUCH AN IMPAIRMENT.—For purposes of paragraph (1)(C):

"(A) An individual meets the requirement of 'being regarded as having such an impairment' if the individual establishes that he or she has been subjected to an action prohibited under this Act because of an actual or perceived physical or mental impairment whether or not the impairment limits or is perceived to limit a major life activity.

"(B) Paragraph (1)(C) shall not apply to impairments that are transitory and minor. A transitory impairment is an impairment with an actual or expected duration of 6 months or less.

"(4) RULES OF CONSTRUCTION REGARDING THE DEFINITION OF DISABILITY.—The definition of 'disability' in paragraph (1) shall be construed in accordance with the following:

"(A) The definition of disability in this Act shall be construed in favor of broad coverage of individuals under this Act, to the maximum extent permitted by the terms of this Act.

"(B) The term 'substantially limits' shall be interpreted consistently with the findings and purposes of the ADA Amendments Act of 2008.

"(C) An impairment that substantially limits one major life activity need not limit other major life activities in order to be considered a disability.

"(D) An impairment that is episodic or in remission is a disability if it would substantially limit a major life activity when active.

"(E)(i) The determination of whether an impairment substantially limits a major life activity shall be made without regard to the ameliorative effects of mitigating measures such as—

"(I) medication, medical supplies, equipment, or appliances, low-vision devices (which do not include ordinary eyeglasses or contact lenses), prosthetics including limbs and devices, hearing aids and cochlear implants or other implantable hearing devices, mobility devices, or oxygen therapy equipment and supplies;

"(II) use of assistive technology;

"(III) reasonable accommodations or auxiliary aids or services; or

"(IV) learned behavioral or adaptive neurological modifications.

"(ii) The ameliorative effects of the mitigating measures of ordinary eyeglasses or contact lenses shall be considered in determining whether an impairment substantially limits a major life activity.

"(iii) As used in this subparagraph—

"(I) the term 'ordinary eyeglasses or contact lenses' means lenses that are intended to fully correct visual acuity or eliminate refractive error; and

"(II) the term 'low-vision devices' means devices that magnify, enhance, or otherwise augment a visual image.".

* * *

SEC. 5.   DISCRIMINATION ON THE BASIS OF DISABILITY.

(a) ON THE BASIS OF DISABILITY.—Section 102 of the Americans with Disabilities Act of 1990 (42 U.S.C. 12112) is amended—

(1) in subsection (a), by striking "with a disability because of the disability of such individual" and inserting "on the basis of disability"; and

(2) in subsection (b) in the matter preceding paragraph (1), by striking "discriminate" and inserting "discriminate against a qualified individual on the basis of disability".

(b) QUALIFICATION STANDARDS AND TESTS RELATED TO UN-CORRECTED VISION.—Section 103 of the Americans with Disabilities Act of 1990 (42 U.S.C. 12113) is amended by redesignating subsections (c) and (d) as subsections (d) and (e), respectively, and inserting after subsection (b) the following new subsection:

"(c) QUALIFICATION STANDARDS AND TESTS RELATED TO UNCORRECTED VISION.—Notwithstanding section 3(4)(E)(ii), a covered entity shall not use qualification standards, employment tests, or other selection criteria based on an individual's uncorrected vision unless the standard, test, or other selection criteria, as used by the covered entity, is shown to be job-related for the position in question and consistent with business necessity."

* * *

SEC. 6. RULES OF CONSTRUCTION.

(a) Title V of the Americans with Disabilities Act of 1990 (42 U.S.C. 12201 et seq.) is amended—

(1) by adding at the end of section 501 the following:

"(e) BENEFITS UNDER STATE WORKER'S COMPENSATION LAWS.—Nothing in this Act alters the standards for determining eligibility for benefits under State worker's compensation laws or under State and Federal disability benefit programs.

"(f) FUNDAMENTAL ALTERATION.—Nothing in this Act alters the provision of section 302(b)(2)(A)(ii), specifying that reasonable modifications in policies, practices, or procedures shall be required, unless an entity can demonstrate that making such modifications in policies, practices, or procedures, including academic requirements in postsecondary education, would fundamentally alter the nature of the goods, services, facilities, privileges, advantages, or accommodations involved.

"(g) CLAIMS OF NO DISABILITY.—Nothing in this Act shall provide the basis for a claim by an individual without a disability that the individual was subject to discrimination because of the individual's lack of disability.

"(h) REASONABLE ACCOMMODATIONS AND MODIFICA-TIONS.—A covered entity under title I, a public entity under title II, and any person who owns, leases (or leases to), or operates a place of public accommodation under title III, need not provide a reasonable accommodation or a reasonable modification to policies, practices, or procedures to an individual who meets the definition of disability in section 3(1) solely under subparagraph (C) of such section."

†